TRY THESE METHODS FOR JUST TWO WEEKS, AND YOU WILL SEE STRIKING CHANGES FOR THE BETTER IN YOUR DOG!

Diet and exercise are the two basics, the foundations on which any training must be built. To help your dog become the loving, healthy, enjoyable pet he was meant to be, the steps set forth in *NUTRITION AND YOUR DOG* are absolutely essential. Simply feeding him the kind of food he really needs will keep him at the peak of health and also shape his behavior to a surprising degree, making later training much easier. It's the best reward you can give your dog!

JOSEPHINE BANKS AND PAUL LOEB, recognized as foremost authorities on animal behavior, have more than 25 years of experience in training thousands of dogs (and their owners) in every subject from feeding an orphaned puppy to exercising an aging canine. They co-authored *The Complete Book of Dog Training, You Can Train Your Cat, Supertraining Your Dog,* and a column on pets for *Parents* magazine. Banks and Loeb were featured in *National Geographic*'s Animal Behavior Series and have lectured on animal behavior and education at ASPCA and Humane Society programs throughout the country.

Books by Josephine Banks and Paul Loeb

The Complete Book of Dog Training
Nutrition and Your Dog
  (*previously published as* Good Dog!)
Supertraining Your Dog
You *Can* Train Your Cat

Published by POCKET BOOKS

NUTRITION
AND YOUR
DOG

Josephine Banks
&
Paul Loeb

POCKET BOOKS

New York   London   Toronto   Sydney   Tokyo

Previously published as *Good Dog!*

 POCKET BOOKS, a division of Simon & Schuster Inc.
1230 Avenue of the Americas, New York, NY 10020

Published by arrangement with the authors
Library of Congress Catalog Card Number: 83-24550

ISBN: 0-671-67868-X

First Pocket Books printing November 1989

10 9 8 7 6 5 4 3 2 1

POCKET and colophon are trademarks of
Simon & Schuster Inc.

Printed in the U.S.A.

TO
Snap   8/21/70–

AND IN MEMORY OF
Plum   10/26/65–2/19/77
Sleepy   12/8/68–1/20/83
Inches   5/8/68–3/7/83

Contents

Contents

NUTRITION AND YOUR DOG

INTRODUCTION

A New Way to Achieving a Perfect Dog

 When, what, and how much you feed and exercise your dog are the keys to a well-behaved, healthy pet. Perhaps it is the very simplicity of these concepts that makes our approach so successful. You have to walk and feed your dog, so why not do it in a way that best serves his interests and yours. Just give our methods a try for a couple of weeks, and you will see striking changes for the better in your dog. No matter how close to perfect you think your dog is, following the steps we advocate will make him better. Even if you are using another book or formal training method, you can supplement them with the feeding and exercise advice we give and achieve even greater success. You've got nothing to lose and everything to gain. There is no effort involved, and our techniques have proven effective over fifteen years with thousands of dogs.

If seeing is believing, see what happens within two weeks of applying the practical techniques we outline:

You will see a changed dog with a healthier coat and skin, a trimmed-up shape, and a better and calmer disposition. Moreover, your dog will be on the way to your goals—to housebreak him, to stop him from chewing furniture and clothing, or to make him refrain from scratching, chewing, and mutilating himself. Most important, you, the owner, will understand your dog's needs and how to better his behavior and health through diet and exercise.

By the way, don't misinterpret our use of the masculine pronoun, he/him, when we refer to dogs generally. We do, of course, use a specific gender designation for any particular dog. But to employ "he or she" would be awkward; "one" would be stilted; and some hybrid form like "s/he" would be bizarre. The neuter "it" is unacceptable to us because dogs are not objects. Too, we do not differentiate between bitch and dog as "she" and "he"; that is esoteric breeding talk to average owners. A dog is a dog, either male or female, as far as they—and we—are concerned.

A TYPICAL EXAMPLE

Not long ago, we received a follow-up letter from one of our clients. "Thank you," the man wrote, "for giving me the key to Natasha's happiness as well as mine."

Natasha was a pure white chow chow who had won Best in Show in two separate American Kennel Club competitions. She had appeared on cable television several times, and her photograph had graced the pages of a number of magazines for dog fanciers. As her owner put it, "Her face, her body, and her fur are her reputation." But last summer, to her owner's dismay, Natasha began scratching obsessively at the right side of her neck. It wasn't long before she developed an area of ugly red sores, both there and on her left paw. Despite her owner's best efforts to distract Natasha, the chow chow licked and chewed at herself constantly.

A veterinarian diagnosed Natasha's malady as "hot spots"—or, in more orthodox medical terms, a form of lick granuloma. This is a fairly common complaint, in which a dog develops one or more highly localized areas that seem irresistibly itchy; the dog will keep on licking, worrying, and scratching at the area even after the hair is worn away and the skin is broken. Accordingly, the veterinarian prescribed cortisone—the standard treatment for a wide variety of inflammations and other skin problems in humans and animals alike.

The cortisone ointment was effective at first—especially on Natasha's paw, where the medication's bad taste deterred her from licking herself. The sores soon healed over. But she continued to scratch at the raw spot at the base of her ruff on the neck, and the lesions failed to heal. Now the vet was puzzled: Were the sores causing the itching, or vice versa?

For the next several months, Natasha was kept off the dog show circuit while her owner tried every remedy the veterinarian suggested—injections, pills, medicinal baths—all to no avail. Finally, remembering that we had helped him train the chow chow as a puppy, her owner called us. Could we give him any insights into why Natasha was mutilating herself?

Most dog trainers adjust and manipulate a dog's behavior through commands, reprimands, and rewards. Our method is entirely different because we believe in adjusting the dog's *entire* environment, not only the feedback he gets from his master. Therefore, when we take on new clients, we always ask to visit them and their pets at their house or apartment. This gives us a chance to see exactly how the dog behaves on his home turf. (Better yet, if a dog is given lessons at home, he's more likely to remember them through simple association—and, therefore, to keep on obeying.)

Of course our clients expect us to put a stop to bad habits, but we see that as only a part of our job. In the words of Matthew Adams, "There are never excuses, but there are always reasons." In other words, we don't believe it's enough simply to discipline a dog—first, we want to find out *why* the dog started misbehaving in the first place.

When we arrived at Natasha's owner's apartment, we noticed right away that the chow chow was slightly overweight—not at all uncommon for a city dog. But this animal was also nervous and high-strung, and apparently much more uncomfortable than the sores alone could account for. Having seen this syndrome many times before, we thought we knew the answer. But we asked a few routine questions, just to rule out any other possibilities.

Yes, her owner was feeding Natasha a diet of dry kibbled food, together with as much water as she wanted to drink. No, he hadn't been exercising her nearly as much since she began scratching; not only was the man ashamed of Natasha's mangy appearance, but he also feared that if she ran around outside too much, the sores of her paw might become infected. Nodding, we explained that the dog's problem was simply too much food and too little exercise: specifically, Natasha was getting entirely the wrong kind of food—and probably too much of it.

The baffled owner couldn't understand how his dog's diet could prompt such chronic itching. But on our advice, he took Natasha off dry dog food and fed her only one and a half cans of moist dog food a day. "That was only two weeks ago," his letter went on. "Natasha seems to be dropping back to her old weight, between forty-nine and fifty-two pounds. She's certainly not emaciated, even though she's eating far less. But most important, her sores have *disappeared!* She's stopped chewing at herself completely, and she's a joy to own again."

The same week this letter arrived, we got a telephone call from an attorney, most of whose clients were in the entertainment field. She had invited a new rock group to stay with her at her Long Island beach house and was afraid that the musicians were having a bad influence on her seven-year-old bichon. Either her long-haired clients were slipping the animal some questionable substance behind her back, or else their heavy-metal practice sessions—or even a whiff of their incense and patchouli—were getting on the bichon's nerves. The dog not only had "hot spots" that he was constantly licking and worrying, but his skin was dry and his coat dull. He slept poorly; in the middle of the night, his owner would often awaken to hear her pet's toenails clicking across the parquet floor. She was in a quandary; these houseguests were potentially important clients. Could we please come by and help the dog adjust to this alternate life-style?

We suspected that the bichon's problem had nothing to do with rock music. We found that every day the attorney was feeding her dog a cup of dry food—which, when moistened, expands to over twice that volume in a dog's stomach—together with a can of food. At our suggestion, she trimmed the dog's daily rations to two-thirds of a can of special low-fat canned dog food and eliminated the dry food completely, even though her veterinarian had advised her that it would "help clean the dog's teeth." That service we provided with a simple rawhide chew-toy.

Within ten days, all of the bichon's problems had disappeared. He slept soundly, even when the musicians had an impromptu concert down on the beach. No longer did he bite or dig at himself; his scabs were quickly healing. And, as a bonus, the dog's weight was swiftly dropping from twenty pounds to a far healthier fifteen pounds, which was more in proportion to his bone structure. "His behavior is greatly improved," his owner wrote us, "and I'm sure this is due to your suggestions for changes in his diet."

Much as the attorney was astonished at the rapid change in her dog's behavior, we weren't. We've seen too many instances in which owners "cured" their dogs' problems in record time, simply by altering the quantity, timing, and type of food they gave their pets. The culprit hasn't always been dry food, of course; sometimes it's been worms or other intestinal parasites that the dog has contracted by eating tidbits off the street. In other, near-fatal cases, garbage has led to serious gastric torsion and pancreatitis. In still other cases, dogs have grown fat and sluggish from "surplus" food sources they've discovered around the house—or in another pet's dish. But virtually every one of these problems has been food-related! Even though we have been working with dogs for more than twenty years, only recently have we come to a full understanding of the enormous importance of diet and exercise in obtaining the results that each client hopes for: a perfect dog.

HOW THIS THEORY BEGAN

All obedience-training lessons we give to owners and their dogs are based on the dynamics of canine pack behavior, as we outlined in *The Complete Book of Dog Training* and in *Supertraining Your Dog*. Obviously those methods were effective, because most owners reported that their dogs were better-behaved and more obedient than ever before. And yet a disturbingly high number of the dogs we worked with seemed to be indulging in markedly abnormal behavior—having as many as six bowel movements a day; gnawing away at their legs, flanks, and base of the tail; scratching until they bled; and remaining mysteriously obese, even after their food intake had been cut in half. Try as we might, we couldn't trace these troubles to any observable interaction between man and beast—and so we could do little more than recommend that these justly worried owners consult veterinarians.

Finally we decided to try out our training theories on a dog of our own. We brought home a lively little weimaraner puppy and named him Plum. As many new dog owners are told to do, we fed him dry kibbled dog food three times a day and kept his water dish brimming so that he could drink his fill. And he *was* thirsty! But to our dismay, Plum seemed impossibly resistant to paper training, much less housebreaking. Despite frequent reprimands, he kept on chewing at the legs of our tables and chairs and ran wild when we took him outside to romp with other dogs in Central Park.

For some reason, the methods our clients had followed successfully weren't working for us. We had heard rumors that weimaraners were a notoriously strong-willed breed and difficult to train, which is why we'd selected Plum in the first place, as a challenge. Was he more of a challenge than we could handle? Or were we doing something wrong?

Then one Friday we discovered that Plum's sack of dry kibble was nearly empty. It was too late to drive downtown to the feed store where hefty fifty-pound bags of dry milled food were sold at a healthy discount. And so, to tide us over the weekend, we bought a few cans of dog food at the local grocery store. When we emptied half a can into Plum's food bowl, he gulped it all down at once, rather than leaving a little to munch later on, as he always did with the kibble. We were slightly concerned that he drank only about half his usual amount of water. But that night he made no mistakes in paper training. The next day, Saturday, he had only a single bowel movement, rather than his usual three. And he was noticeably calmer, less destructive and hyperactive.

But *why?* The switch to canned food seemed to be the only possible variable. As an experiment, we went back to the grocery and bought another dozen cans—and kept Plum on the new diet. To our delighted surprise, he stayed housebroken and stopped chewing the furniture, completely on his own. But outside, he was still a problem, constantly running off by himself and refusing to come when called.

That willful behavior didn't change until the New York City Police Department started a crackdown and began handing out summonses to owners who let their dogs run off the leash. Then if Plum accompanied us to Central Park, we had to have him heeling close by our sides and couldn't let him play with other "outlaw" dogs. To make sure he was still getting enough exercise, we trained him to jump low hurdles, then, as he grew larger, fire hydrants and garbage cans. This was a trick basically—but it was also a quick exercise that let him work off extra energy and gave his muscles a real workout.

After about a month of being restricted to these controlled, closely supervised exercises, Plum calmed down even more. For no apparent reason, he was suddenly far more obedient and attentive, willing to pay attention to his other lessons. On the street he heeled perfectly, and even when taken off the leash he stayed right by us and *always* came when called.

We sensed we were onto something. But since Plum was now responding exactly as our clients said *their* dogs did, we weren't precisely sure what had caused the change. Had he just been going through a phase? We decided to buy another dog and find out.

When we bought Inches, our first Maltese spaniel, we started him right off with canned dog food, sprinkling his daily meals with wheat germ for added nourishment. Because Inches was so small, tipping the scales at a mere nine pounds, we were never even tempted to let him play with other strange dogs. Simply for convenience, we often carried him up and down stairs to go out, and so he developed a real bond with us. That, we assumed, was the main reason his training proceeded without a hitch, with no relapses or stubbornness. But then, he had been on Plum's diet-and-exercise regimen from the very start.

When we brought home Snap and Sleepy, our other two Maltese spaniels, they were six weeks and six months old, respectively. But the age difference didn't seem to matter; we put them on the same program as Plum and Inches, and they responded perfectly. But pleased as we were with our own four dogs, we still didn't insist that our clients follow a similar regimen. After all, many of the top dog experts were recommending that puppies be allowed to "self-feed" on dry food as often as they liked. And the dry foods are complete and balanced and good for dogs of any age— it says so right on the label!

Certainly our clients had plenty of reasonable explanations for the problems they called upon us to solve. If a dog was jumpy and restless, it had to be because he'd been cooped up in an apartment all day. If he chewed up the sofa pillows or relieved himself behind the couch, wasn't that a gesture of resentment? Naturally, if he was chewing himself raw, it was a sign of boredom. And, after all, weren't some particular breeds, such as terriers and poodles, just naturally nervous and high-strung?

We began to wonder, after seeing Plum "grow out of" a wide variety of very similar problems. So we began to explore exactly *how* variables of diet and exercise could alter a dog's behavior. Was the chronic yappiness of small dogs not so much a matter of breeding or genetics but simply too much food for these small-bodied dogs? Were many of the "emotional" problems that dogs exhibit—hyperactivity, whining, outbreaks of chewing, lapses in housebreaking—also a direct consequence of bad eating habits?

We aren't veterinarians or nutritionists, but fortunately we have access to a number of other professionals who work with animals. If we aren't sure how to handle a problem that crops up with one of our clients' pets or one of our own four dogs, we research the subject as best we can and then call one of our expert friends for an opinion. Then, after considering all the facts, we do what seems most appropriate, in light of our own knowledge of canine behavior. And every so often, we saw a direct link between how a dog was acting and what he was being fed. Again and again, many of the "typical" hassles that people encountered in dog training cropped up in households that employed traditional feeding methods.

THE SOURCE OF THE PROBLEM

We discovered that when it comes to feeding their dogs, all too many owners are blinded by myths and misconceptions. At one extreme are those who insist that their dogs are practically human and so should get along just fine on the same food that the rest of the family is eating. The irony here, of course, is that most human meals aren't all that nourishing. The heat of cooking breaks down a number of important vitamins and proteins, and, unless you do your shopping with great care in the first place, you may not even be starting out with all the nutrients you really need. Moreover, human and canine digestive tracts are somewhat different. What may be healthy enough and appropriate for you—for example, three square meals a day—may be all wrong for your dog.

At the other extreme are the owners who assume there is a vast biological gap between themselves and their pets. They consider their dogs an utterly different species, incomprehensible and inscrutable, and these people don't use common sense about their dogs but are quick to follow the advice of any self-proclaimed "expert" who appears in the daily paper or on the radio or television. Oddly, many health-conscious people read books and magazines about diet and exercise, but most of what they know about their dogs' nutritional needs is drawn from TV commercials and the fine print on the back of dog food containers.

To be fair, commercial dog food companies have gone to some trouble to develop well-balanced, nutritious products (a subject we'll cover in more depth in Chapter 3). But dogs don't buy dog food—owners do, and so, not too surprisingly, most dog food brands stress features that appeal mostly to *people,* such as economy and convenience. "Rich hearty flavor" means simply that a dog will gulp the food down and lick his bowl clean, with no waste. Sales points and advertising claims like this have little to do with the dog's long-term nutrients; yet all too often such well-intentioned but basically erroneous claims are accepted without question by trusting dog owners.

Unfortunately, in some cases it's been easier for us to give directions than to explain. In a few seemingly "impossible" cases of canine misbehavior, we told the dogs' owners to change their pets' diets as a last resort. We worked on the basic concept, refining it over several years and, after a great deal of research and application, finally put together the outline of a program that's successful for every breed of dog, from puppyhood to old age.

Not that our original Pack Theory isn't valid—it's

still the basis for all of our obedience training. But owner/dog interaction has to rest on a foundation of proper diet and exercise. So to a large extent, then, our previous books are really later installments that ought to be read *after* this one.

"Since I've changed his food, he's been so wonderful to be with" is a statement we've heard over and over. On the right diet, a formerly yapping, aggressive, over-active dog becomes vastly calmer and easier to live with. But, to be honest, not all our clients are delighted with the changes in their pets' behavior. After we helped one hyperactive French poodle calm down, his owner thought that the dog was "depressed." Another client charged that we had "broken my dog's spirit." Of course, if you have no other dogs to compare him with, it's all too easy to become accustomed to your own animal's abnormal behavior. Remember, though, that a happy pet doesn't have to behave like a jumping jack or be constantly on the go. Of course there *are* times when your dog should be alert, excited, and energetic, and (as you'll see in Chapter 8) that's exactly what outdoor exercise is all about.

At first glance, though, our program seems all too simple. New clients often are skeptical that such a broad spectrum of canine misery can be remedied by just a few simple changes. "Since I've switched our beagle to canned dog food, he's been really good about housebreaking. Back when he was eating the semi-moist food, he was drinking an awful lot and urinating day and night—and not always outside either, where he was supposed to. Why is it that vets recommend semi-moist and dry food in the first place?"

In other words, if our method is so effective, why

haven't you *already* heard about it from your veterinarian? One possible explanation comes from Dr. Mildred Seelig, the editor of the *Journal of the American College of Nutrition*. She has complained that it's "possible for medical students to get almost no training in nutrition except for what they're taught in biochemistry about acute deficiency nutritional states such as beriberi." Dr. Seelig advises that doctors—and by extension, veterinarians—who are concerned about nutrition should "keep learning on their own, because nutrition, like other fields in medicine, is expanding rapidly." We understand that to mean that even those who have specifically studied nutrition may be behind the times.

The reason the entire field is "expanding rapidly" is simply that the science of nutrition, compared with other branches of medicine, is still in its infancy. Doctors now know that dietary imbalances can cause a wide variety of problems in humans, including low blood sugar (hypoglycemia) and hyperactivity and learning disablities in children. Recent studies have established even more convincing one-to-one links between diet and behavior, showing how the food any animal ingests is metabolized into various chemical compounds, which in turn affect the body's ability to respond to the environment. But these discoveries have been slow in coming. Since it's not possible to experiment on human beings, the vast majority of nutrition-deprivation studies have been done on laboratory rats and mice and, to a lesser extent, on dogs. But again, these are *deprivation* experiments, focusing on what happens when an animal's system is deprived of a single nutrient.

By this kind of trial-and-error methodology, the Food and Drug Administration has established a Recommended Daily Allowance (RDA) for scores of vitamins, minerals, and trace elements. These are the *minimum* doses that are required to maintain health. Yet the exact amount of nutrition humans really need for *good* health is still a matter of controversy. Some nutritionists and health-food experts insist that the government's RDAs represent only a fraction of what the body needs to sustain itself and are not adequate for really robust health.

As far as canine nutrition is concerned, scientists have established the bare minimum it takes to keep a dog from falling ill; below that point, specific nutritional deficiencies can result in a wide range of health problems from minor skin rashes and cystitis (the formation of abscesses beneath the skin) to birth defects and bone abnormalities in older dogs. But so far virtually no research has been done on the *positive* side. That is, what kind of diet does a dog need to achieve the *best* possible health and happiness?

Our own experience indicates that the sheer *quantity* of a dog's food has considerable effect on his ability to digest it all. But, again, little or no research has been devoted to the slow, long-term effects of overeating on a dog's system. Veterinarians warn you not to overfeed your dog because of a sometimes fatal side effect called gastric torsion, in which the dog's stomach capsizes and twists itself shut like a plastic bag. But a vet is less likely to look for dietary deficiencies that have been *caused* by too much food.

To make your veterinarian's job even trickier, it's easy for dietary problems to masquerade as other maladies. Certain nutrients must be precisely balanced before the body can use them properly. Thus if a dog isn't getting enough phosphorus, he won't be able to absorb enough calcium. If his bones become brittle and soft, it may *appear* that his diet is weak in calcium, while the phosphorus deficiency is the real culprit. Moreover, many diet-related conditions and diseases take a long time to develop, which makes it nearly impossible for an owner to pinpoint when the trouble actually began.

Worse still, any one dietary deficiency seldom produces only a single symptom. An overfed dog may tend toward obesity and *also* display a compulsion to chew, together with lethargy, skin rashes, irritability, sleeplessness, arthritis, and diabetes. Rather than trace all these conditions and diseases to their common origin, a harried veterinarian is far more likely to treat them as entirely separate problems.

In many cases, such as Natasha the chow chow, the cause-and-effect relationship is not always obvious, so to save time, a veterinarian often prescribes a number of treatments at once. Then, if the dog's condition improves, it may appear the problem's been licked. But while diet-related problems can be *treated* successfully, they can't be completely *cured* unless the underlying dietary cause is corrected.

TURNING THE PROBLEM AROUND

Most nutritional studies on dogs have been done in a clinic, kennel, or laboratory. Many researchers have stated that there's no way to extrapolate the exact diet needed by a pet dog living at home. We disagree. In fact, in the next few chapters, we'll show you exactly how to do this, because all of *our* "studies" have taken place in the homes of pet dogs. Animals behave quite differently on their home turf than in the strange environment of a clinic or veterinarian's office. So, because we make "house calls," we tend to see habitual behavior patterns that other professionals never get to see. An owner may swear that his pet eats nothing but ordinary dog food at regular times. But often we'll watch this same person absentmindedly hand his dog a scrap of food from his lunch, or we'll see the dog steal a morsel of cheese spread and cracker off a low coffee table. And in the country and suburbs, where dogs are often allowed to run free, they can often gobble down any amount of garbage without their owners being any the wiser.

When food is the *only* variable in a dog's life, the cause-and-effect link is obvious—and often dramatic. One of our clients complained that his otherwise well-behaved golden retriever had suddenly begun chewing a throw rug. We asked if the dog's diet had been changed in any way. After some thought, the owner finally remembered that he had stopped giving his dog a powdered vitamin supplement in favor of a more convenient liquid dosage. Just as an experiment, we asked him to go back to powdered vitamins for a week or so. To his astonishment, the retriever promptly stopped chewing.

This kind of dramatic reaction to a minor change of diet is only too common in the dogs we work with. The real challenge, of course, is understanding *why* these drastic changes take place. Did the liquid vitamin leave the dog with some unfulfilled hankering? If the patient were human, of course, you could ask; with a dog, we can only guess.

Doctors and psychiatrists agree that, among people, being able to talk out our troubles is an important safety valve that gives a boost to mental *and* physical health. But your dog's communication is limited mainly to body language. If he's bothered by indigestion or a too full stomach, he can complain only by whining or whimpering. If what he eats stimulates his bowels or bladder, he's likely to start gnawing on furniture to distract himself. The vivid stimulation of chewing tends to drown out the vague, unpleasant sensations he feels from within.

Of course, if you've already taught him not to chew on things, his inhibitions only compound the problem. With no other outlet for his nervous energy, sooner or later he'll start chewing on himself—an act which hasn't yet been forbidden him. Thus the veterinarian is presented with yet another case of lick granuloma.

But as these "motivations" for bad behavior are gradually eliminated, your dog will become far more responsive to positive training. Free of internal distractions, not having to relearn what *not* to do, he's able to pay more attention to what you, his owner, *do* want of him. Certainly he'll be happier spending his energies in play, training, and exercise than in combating discomfort and anxiety. A healthy dog is *eager* to learn. Traditionally, trainers have used food rewards as a means of getting their point across, but we've discovered that a dog will learn much faster and more thoroughly *without* any rewards at all.

These few case histories (and you'll be reading quite a few more) might lead you to think we've discovered a magic formula to whisk away all the problems that dog owners encounter. In a sense, we have—but there's actually nothing magical about it. Proper diet takes effect so very quickly because your dog's body is incredibly efficient. Not only does your dog age faster than you do, but his metabolism and digestion work a good deal faster. Therefore, once given the nourishment it needs, your dog's system quickly moves to repair itself. And once his physical needs are being answered, many of the apparently "psychological" problems tend to disappear. Apparently stubborn dogs housebreak themselves, sometimes overnight. Annoying, destructive habits like chewing and leaping about go away by themselves. And lessons you've been repeating for days suddenly take hold.

"A few months ago," one client wrote us, "I called you—for the second time—about our springer spaniel and his chewing problem. We took him off dry food, as you advised us to, and put him on one of the canned, moist brands. His chewing stopped miraculously, except for one incident—but *only* one—two months later. Best of all, he really likes the new food. If we had only followed your advice in the first place, we'd have saved ourselves a lot of trouble and repair bills."

Now that people are more and more aware of the importance of diet and exercise in their own lives, they're better able to understand the importance of these to their dogs as well. Until now, most owners have thought of dog food as simply a means of satisfying their pets' hunger—and perhaps a means of expressing love. In reality, though, food is a surprisingly effective tool that can improve not only your dog's disposition but the sheen of his coat and even his susceptibility to fleas!

With all the books on human fitness, we feel it's time

for one on dog fitness. But this isn't intended as a technical treatise on nutrition. Instead, it's a *practical* guidebook to certain aspects of your dog's diet and exercise requirements as they affect his behavior and health—all based on what we've learned from direct observation of hundreds of dogs and their owners. In the following pages, we set forth a comprehensive program that can be "customized" to fit the needs of *any* individual pet, from a just-weaned Chihuahua to a pregnant Great Dane. We have examined reports on eating habits of wild dogs (including hyenas, dingoes, and feral packs) to see how these animals feed themselves and to recognize what instincts they carry over into domestic life. The result is a state-of-the-art regimen that takes into account your pet's individual size, life-style, habits, and bone structure.

As we suggested before, diet and exercise don't constitute a cure-all for *every* problem your dog may have. But they are the two basics, the foundation on which any training must be built. To help your dog become the loving, healthy, enjoyable pet he was meant to be, the steps set forth in the following chapters are absolutely essential. Simply feeding him the kind of food he really needs (rather than what advertisements and folklore might have you believe) will keep him at the peak of health and also shape his behavior to a surprising degree, making later training much easier. All in all, our program will save you time and money: almost immediately you'll spend fewer hours in corrections and cleanups; and in the long run, your dog's improved health will save you hundreds of dollars in veterinary bills.

Perhaps the very best part of our method is that it

takes no more effort to feed a dog right than it does to feed him wrong. Once you've done a little planning, there isn't much talent or work involved. Or, as one of our clients put it, "My dog has to eat, regardless—so I might as well feed him to my own advantage."

Exercise, too, has to be tailored to your dog's specific needs; too much activity and he'll be hungry all the time, eating more than is good for him or convenient for you. Besides, we've seen too many dogs exhausted or even injured by sporadic, uncontrolled "workouts." For some breeds, the wrong sorts of tricks can be just as harmful as no exercise at all. (For example, a low-slung dachsund shouldn't be asked to sit up. Strenuous actions such as jumping should be avoided with any heavier breeds with a tendency to hip dysplasia.)

Moderate, *regular* exercise is the way to go; it will not only keep your dog's various systems in good shape, but it will also implicitly teach him obedience and keep him from picking up bad habits. We give specific guidelines for the kinds of play/exercise your dog can safely enjoy—from the time he's a puppy until he's fifteen, or even older.

We'll cover special dietary "troubleshooting" for specific problems like bad breath, constipation, and flatulence—as well as special supplements for pregnant and nursing dogs. Finally, we'll outline the changes in diet and activity you should make as your pet grows older, and we'll discuss certain health problems that geriatric dogs can easily overcome—*if* you notice the symptoms in time to get proper veterinary care and make the necessary diet changes. (For example, aging dogs are particularly susceptible to kidney trouble, which requires plenty of fluids and a reduction of protein in the diet.)

It's true that your dog is a different species of mammal, but that doesn't mean you have to make allowances for his behavior. All he asks is that you tailor his food, training, and play to suit the demands of his particular physiology. In good measure, that means harnessing the instincts and behavior patterns that every domestic dog has developed over millions of years of evolution. And the best place to begin is by understanding how the canine digestive system has adapted to the rigors of life in the wild.

1

Your Dog's Eating Habits and How They Evolved

 The one-celled amoeba still gets its nourishment by wrapping its food in a protoplasmic embrace. But higher forms of life have developed more complicated ways of meeting their nutritional needs— ways that have a very direct bearing on whether they're suitable as pets. If you want to keep a koala bear, anteater, or flamingo, you'd better be able to stock up on fresh eucalyptus leaves (for the koala), live termites and beetle grubs (for the anteater), or fresh shrimp (which a flamingo needs to maintain its livid pink plumage). In fact, most of this planet's most beautiful, exotic, and appealing animal species don't do well in captivity simply because they require diets that are much too complex and specialized for the average pet owner to provide.

It's obviously easier—and far less expensive—to co-exist with an animal who doesn't demand food that's still alive or freshly picked. But because your family dog *is* so simple to feed, it's easy to overlook the fact that he, too, has been shaped just as precisely by evolution as have the koala, anteater, and flamingo, whose body shapes are engineered to assist in food hunting. So is your dog "shaped" to help him find his next meal, but until you understand exactly how, many of his mealtime actions may seem a mite bizarre, if not downright baffling.

Most dog owners are aware that their pets evolved from a predatory wolflike animal. Indeed, most breeds of dogs still have fairly long legs and narrow paws to help them run faster. As you know, your dog's a good runner and can sustain short bursts of speed. Outdoors, he delights in prowling through the underbrush where other small animals and birds tend to shelter. One veterinarian has speculated that a dog's long, floppy ears evolved to protect his ear canals from twigs and branches during the chase. We disagree. All wild canines have upright-standing ears, as do many domestic breeds. Long, floppy ears are a fairly recent genetic anomaly, a trait deliberately bred by dog fanciers. A dog's eyesight isn't especially keen, but, then, when a bird or rabbit is hiding in long grass, vision isn't much help. Far more practical are a good sense of smell, to detect the odor of a frightened animal, and good ears, to detect its rustles and the noise of its breathing.

Not surprisingly, then, smell and hearing are your dog's keenest senses. By comparison, the human nose is laughably ineffective, when you consider that a dog can detect a drop of urine dissolved in a gallon of water.

The well-known pack behavior of dogs and wolves is yet another survival tactic that evolved, we believe, mainly for food-gathering purposes. Being in a pack actually allows these canines to hunt down larger prey animals. Consider the fox, a solitary hunter, by comparison. Some species of foxes are no larger than well-fed house cats, and this relatively small size, together with independent hunting habits, effectively limits the size of their prey to animals smaller than themselves. Foxes feed most often on rabbits, birds, small rodents, and even insects.

Coyotes are substantially larger predators, ranging in weight from about thirty up to sixty-five pounds. Moreover, coyotes often hunt in pairs, and this cooperative stalking enables them to bring down animals as large as sheep, much to the annoyance of ranchers. Dogs—and their close relatives, wolves—hunt in even larger groups of up to a dozen and so are able to kill deer, elk, and other quadrupeds *larger* than themselves. (In the days of the Old West, early settlers reported a strain of "buffalo wolves," named after their favorite prey.)

Thus, pack behavior exerts a kind of leverage on the environment, helping ensure the survival of a species. It's a simple equation: the larger the prey an animal can feed on, the less likely it is to go hungry.

GULP, DON'T CHEW

You'll notice that a dog's mouth isn't exactly built for leisurely chewing. Your dog sports a set of forty-two teeth, the front ones shaped for cutting and tearing, the heavy back molars for crushing bone and connective tissue. These enameled weapons, plus a very strong bite, enable him to bolt food in large chunks. And in the wild, dogs habitually tear their food apart, cutting off large chunks and "wolfing" them down. A dog seldom bothers to chew his food unless it's too big to gulp down. His stomach does the "chewing" for him, by churning the food mechanically.

This gorging, of course, is an inbred trait, with obvious survival advantages. Wild dogs can't be sure of eating on a regular schedule. A day or two, perhaps even a week or more, can pass between kills. Whenever food *is* available, the dog will eat until his hunger is satisfied—and then keep right on eating, cramming down as much as he can. In one instance, a *New York Times* reporter saw a pack of African hyenas bring down a wildebeest in the early evening. By daybreak, there was nothing left of the wildebeest's carcass except horns and hooves—which are composed of indigestible chiton, the same material that makes up our hair and fingernails.

Our Maltese, Sleepy, weighed less than six pounds, but later in life he developed a ravenous appetite, triggered by an overproduction of cortisone by his adrenal glands. One afternoon when we were out, he got hold of a raw steak we had left defrosting in the kitchen; by the time we returned home, he was sitting in the center of the living room floor, panting, his tongue hanging nearly to the floor. As soon as we saw the torn aluminum foil, we knew what had happened. Hoping to make him throw up the excess, we forced open his mouth and stuck a finger down his throat. Unbelievably, the chunks of steak were backed up clear to his esophagus! How he was able to breathe we'll never know. To make sure his intestines weren't blocked, we took him down to the street and gave him a suppository. Within minutes, he defecated—indicating that he'd be able to pass the steak on through. And sure enough, within two days, he was vigorously eating his regular meals with undiminished craving.

Your dog's sloppy table manners are also a part of his evolutionary heritage. Since packs are composed of three or more animals, each one *has* to eat fast or risk losing out entirely. To be sure he gets his fair share, a wild dog will often tear loose a morsel and drag it some distance from the carcass where he can finish it off in private. If you give your dog something he can't chew up and swallow quickly—a bone, say, or a particularly hard dog biscuit—he may well remove it from his dish and carry it off to finish elsewhere.

That's not to say that wild dogs can afford to eat at leisure. Any pack that lingered over unrefrigerated meat would risk food poisoning, and eating quickly reduces the risk of meeting other animals attracted by the scent, who might want to share the meal. (This is basically why dogs bury bones: to clean up the site of their "kill" and to preserve hard-to-chew morsels they can't eat right away.)

It would seem, then, that your dog is a born carnivore, designed by nature to subsist on an all-meat diet. But this brings us to the first paradox in canine physiology: a pure meat diet is *not* enough for your dog! Fed nothing but filet mignon, a dog would eventually die of malnutrition—just as you would.

Zoologists commonly classify all animals into three categories: *herbivorous* (plant and seed eaters), *carnivorous* (meat eaters), and *omnivorous* (able to eat and digest both plant and animal tissue). But, in reality, very few animal species fit neatly and *entirely* into either of the first two categories. Biologists point out that a "vegetarian" cow, horse, or sheep actually consumes significant amounts of animal protein, in the form of insects and other small organisms that happen to be clinging to the leaves and grasses upon which it grazes. Hungry foxes, wolves, and coyotes have been known to munch on fruits and berries; and these animals—as well as wild dogs—might best be classified as "hidden" omnivores.

True, their digestive tracts don't have the enzymes to digest fresh fruit and vegetables. But in most cases they don't need to! Whenever wild dogs in a pack bring down an animal, they begin by eating the stomach, intestines, and other internal organs. Most animals that wild dogs prey on—deer, rabbits, birds—are plant eaters, whose innards are filled with partly digested vegetation that a dog's stomach can handle with no trouble. That's why when a dog munches grass, he's doing it strictly to get roughage or to make himself vomit—it's not for nourishment. He never *needed* to develop the digestive enzymes that break down vegetable matter from scratch because his ancestors let other animals seek out the vegetable portion of their diets—and even begin the digestive process!

After devouring the innards of their prey, wild dogs go on to consume as much of the carcass as they can, including the sinews, cartilage, tendons, bones, and other connective tissue. Different body organs concentrate different levels and mixtures of specific nutrients, so, by eating as much as he can, a wild dog manages to achieve something close to a "balanced" meal.

After gorging himself, a wild dog will wander off and usually fall asleep, devoting all his body energies to the process of digestion. His stomach and intestines shift into high gear, trying to derive as much nourishment as possible. But this brings us to another paradox: even though your dog's system is superbly equipped to handle huge meals, this accelerated digestion isn't particularly efficient; the more food a dog's small intestine has to process, the fewer nutrients it's able to extract.

A wild dog is able to process most of the quick-dissolving sugars and carbohydrates he has eaten because these have been partially digested for him in the stomach of the prey animal that he ate. He will store a good deal of his food energy as glycerin or body fat. Both will be metabolized later to keep the dog's system running between "meals." In the wild, a dog may well feel hunger, but he won't be obsessed by it. Until food is actually present, the digestive tract simply shuts down, letting the dog direct all his attention and energies into seeking new prey. This leads to yet another surprise of canine behavior: hunting and hunger are two entirely different drives, and only coincidentally related.

EATING VS. APPETITE

If your dog dashes happily after birds, cats, and squirrels, it's usually out of a sense of adventurous play or territorial protectiveness. But unless a dog is encouraged to pursue other creatures, his hunting instinct will more or less atrophy. After all, hunting is a pack activity, since it takes more than one dog to bring down a sizable animal. And as your dog's master, you're essentially his pack leader; if *you're* not doing any hunting, he's not about to either, no matter how hungry he gets.

Stumpy, a schnauzer that Jo owned when she was a

child, is a fine illustration of how deeply separate these two instincts really are. Jo lived in a rural area where a dog could wander for days and not cover the same ground twice. By day, Stumpy used to pal around with a springer spaniel, and together they would hunt and kill small animals—ones considered pests, such as groundhogs. The actual "killing technique" *does* seem to be instinctive: if you toss a soft rag doll to a puppy, he'll often shake it vigorously to "kill" it. This is how a wild dog dispatches a small animal—he seizes the prey just behind the neck and shakes it hard, fracturing the spine. Stumpy had never learned to hunt from his mother or littermates, yet all of his kills had died quickly and cleanly, of a broken neck. How did Jo know? Because Stumpy would usually carry his trophies home and dump them on the doorstep.

Although a dog enjoys chasing other animals, or hunting, on his own he won't necessarily make the connection between quarry and food. That's an association that has to be taught by his mother or other animals in his pack. Neither Stumpy nor his spaniel sidekick ever thought of eating what they killed. Every evening, Stumpy would return home for his daily meal—two cans of dog food mixed with a can of water. Despite his vestigial hunting drive, your modern dog is really quite different from his wild ancestors. Several thousand years of controlled breeding have resulted in genetic changes—the squat legs of a bulldog, for example, and the wall eyes of a pug—that natural selection would never have allowed. But down through the centuries, a more subtle form of natural selection has taken place: dogs who got along well with families were fed and pampered. Ill-tempered, difficult dogs were often thrown out of the house either to perish of starvation or be hunted down as a threat to sheep and cattle. Thus, your modern-day dog has been *bred* to be friendly; it's part of his heritage.

Along the way, of course, the dog's digestive system also has undergone certain adaptations. For centuries, pet dogs have been fed scraps from the table or allowed to munch on bones and offal flung out behind the kitchen. (Any movie epic set in medieval days usually has a few canine "extras" scrounging food from the table of the king or peasant or Viking or soldier.) Any individual dogs who couldn't get by on this haphazard scraps-and-discards diet didn't survive to bear healthy puppies. So dogs have been bred to be almost as omnivorous as their human masters.

There are times, of course—*rare* times—when a dog's appetite will simply vanish. If he's displaying any physical symptoms—for example, fever, diarrhea, lassitude, obvious discomfort, or excessive sleepiness—that's a clear signal to take him to the veterinarian to discover what's wrong. But if he seems healthy enough, the cause is probably emotional: fear or guilt over recent misbehavior (if you've just reprimanded him, he'll feel a bit uneasy in your presence). Or he may just be jealously distracted by the presence of another animal or human visitor in *his* house.

Most people have heard of Pavlov's famous experiment in which he conditioned dogs to salivate at the sound of a bell. Your dog's "hunger" is largely a matter of just this kind of conditioning. If you feed him at a given time each day, his stomach will begin contracting and secreting gastric juices at that specific hour. Then, if a dog is drooling, does that mean he's hungry? Not necessarily. Every dog naturally drips saliva when his mouth is open—on a hot day or when he's panting after exercise. (If you want to protect the floor or carpet, give your pet a special rug all his own that he can lie—and drool—on.)

The problem is, your dog will be on the lookout for food before *and* after his regular mealtime, whether or not he's actually hungry. One summer, we went on a fifteen-week camping trip with our four dogs, Plum, Sleepy, Inches, and Snap. They had all grown up in the city, where they'd had to live a highly disciplined, highly structured existence. As many dog owners do, we found it enjoyable to project our own wishes and explore the wilderness, without leashes or other restrictions. But from the first campsite to the last, all that our four "explorers" were interested in were garbage dumps and other campers who thought they were cute enough to feed.

But isn't it true that a dog's digestive system shuts down between meals? Yes, but his *hopes* don't!

Feral animals don't get all their food by hunting; they supplement their diets by scavenging—raiding garbage cans, eating dead animals, and stealing prey from smaller, weaker predators. Scavenging enables any species to get by when normal prey is scarce. And, from an evolutionary standpoint, it must be pretty effective, because in nature scavengers far outnumber predators. For every shark or tarpon, there are several thousand flounders; for every osprey or sea eagle, a skyful of seagulls.

In some species, in fact, it's not always easy to tell where preying leaves off and scavenging begins. An arctic fox will often follow a polar bear for days, waiting for it to kill a seal; when the bear eats, the fox eats too. A coyote will often follow a herd of deer, waiting to pick off sick or dying animals. The coyote is a shameless, notorious scavenger—and has extended its original range in the Western United States north to Alaska and eastward to New England in the face of growing urbanization and nearly two centuries of trapping, poisoning, and shooting by indignant farmers. And genetically, a coyote is extremely similar, if not identical, to a dog; in fact, dogs and coyotes have been known to interbreed and spawn "coydogs."

Though pack hunting by definition is a team effort, scavenging is a solitary activity—finders keepers!—and so it's a behavior trait that tends to persist. Even a well-fed (*and* well-nourished—they aren't the same thing) pet will try to take food away from a weaker animal—namely, you. Does your dog come to the table when you're eating and give you a pitiful, soulful stare? You should know that in canine body language, a stare is an aggressive challenge. When you give in and slip a begging dog the treat he wanted, you've abdicated your authority—in his eyes, at least. That's why a begging dog so quickly gets to be an insufferable pest; he thinks *he's* in charge because he's been able to make you give up food that he knows is yours. (The fact that you never swipe food from *his* bowl only proves that you're afraid of him!)

Your dog also will nose his way down the street, poking his snout into garbage cans and slurping up discarded tidbits, unless you are kind enough to teach him not to (more about this in Chapter 7). But this brings us to yet another paradox of canine behavior. There's no doubt that a dog *can* distinguish the difference between a fresh veal scallopini and week-old salami rotting in the street. But he'll eat both with equal gusto. If a dog's sense of smell is so acute, how can he manage to enjoy such vile-smelling things?

SMELL VS. TASTE

It's clear that dogs really don't like certain aromas. They are definitely repelled by any bitter, caustic odor such as woodsmoke, vinegar, ammonia, and powdered detergent. Many dogs will beg for a sip of wine or liquor just because *you're* having some, only to back off after one quick whiff. (Your dog's urine also has a particularly acrid smell—and it's no coincidence that he uses this aroma to warn other animals not to trespass on his territory.)

When it comes to the smells dogs *prefer,* however, things get a bit trickier. A dog's sense of smell is so sharp, it's hard for human experimenters to be sure that any odor is "pure" enough to give meaningful results. From our own observation, we think that a dog is more interested in a *variety* of scents than in just how "good" or "bad" any one smells. It's important to remember that your dog's nose evolved to help in scavenging as well as in hunting. Therefore, the more exotic a given substance smells, the more likely it is to *be* different, and to provide him with a whole new set of nutrients. In other words, seeking out a wide variety of smells could help "balance" a wild dog's diet—and thus have important survival advantages.

Because humans chew for a fairly long time, we tend to take our time over meals and savor our food in a way that dogs don't—or don't bother to. Many a dog owner has offered a pet a choice morsel only to watch in disappointment as the dog sniffs at it, then gulps it down without tasting it. Your dog's sense of smell (which tells him, basically, where the food is) has evolved far beyond his sense of taste (which tells him only if food is blatantly unpalatable). As long as his smell is operating like a radar, helping him locate the widest possible range of nourishment, then for sheer survival, taste is just a waste of time. The faster he can gulp something down, the faster he can be off sniffing for his next morsel—as you'll quickly discover if you ever decide to "appease" a begging dog.

There's one big drawback, though, to this sniff-and-taste-later approach: interesting odors will prompt your dog to swallow a wide range of items that he can't digest effectively. Rich and spicy foods and—particularly in older dogs—milk may lead to diarrhea; while foods his stomach and intestines can't break down (notably, fruits and raw vegetables) pass through untouched.

One evening, we arrived home a bit later than expected. Our four dogs had been waiting long enough, and we didn't want to give them any excuse to break training. So, without even stepping into the apartment, we let the dogs out and started downstairs. The Hispanic elevator operator glanced at Inches, laughed, and said, *"puerco."* We suddenly noticed that Inches really did look as fat as a pig. Outside, Inches quickly defecated; his stool was deep green. His belly was huge and hard and he felt heavy as lead.

We hurried back upstairs to put the other dogs inside and to phone our veterinarian and warn her that we were on our way with an emergency. As we dashed again toward the elevator, Jo kicked against a paper bag and green pellets scattered out onto the floor. It was the new bag of dry guinea-pig pellets we'd left in the kitchen. But then it was in the hall, only about two-thirds full. The connection was obvious, especially since Inches loved grain products. When we called the vet back, she laughed and agreed that we didn't have to bring Inches in unless he developed other problems or symptoms. As long as he kept on defecating with no trouble, that was a good sign.

To make sure he didn't gulp water and put any more stress on his distended stomach, we gave Inches ice cubes to lick and took him down to the street as often as he wanted. Over the next day he went through half a dozen trays of ice cubes, urinated a lot, and defecated hard and green. But within two days, he was back to normal—partly because of the way a dog's digestive tract speeds up to handle such overloads.

The moral of this story is an important point that we'll be emphasizing throughout this book: *hunger and nourishment are two separate and independent factors.* Your dog's appetite is *not* an accurate gauge of how well you're feeding him. A hungry dog is seldom an underfed one; nor is a plump, satisfied pet necessarily getting all the nourishment he really needs. (As we'll explain in Chapter 5, it's probably healthier to keep your dog just a bit below the "ideal" weight your veterinarian recommends.)

A second moral, of course, is that a dog's nose is sensitive enough to detect odors emanating from many types of containers. A dog will avoid most human medications, such as cold capsules and sedatives, because they have an extremely bitter taste. But to make these substances more palatable, manufacturers often use pleasant-tasting coatings that quickly dissolve once the medicine reaches the stomach. To a dog, this "sugar coating" is an enticing aroma. Because dogs have a relatively low body weight, it's very easy for them to overdose on "adult-strength" medications, and suffer severe gastric upset, coma, and even death. Remember that even a child-proof container of hard plastic won't withstand a few minutes of determined chewing. It's a good idea to keep *all* dry foodstuffs, pills, and bottles in cabinets high off the floor or behind doors that can be latched.

2
Your Dog's Nutritional Requirements

 Forget trying to simulate the diet your pet might eat if he were living like his ancestors or present-day wild cousins; you won't be able to provide it. Where are you going to find the carcass of a freshly killed prey animal in our prepackaged, supermarket society? Besides, you and your dog will be far better off if you give him one of the commercial diets available today for domestic dogs. These specially formulated foods are superior to natural fare. They take into account your dog's nutritional needs, as well as his weaknesses; they provide better and more consistent nourishment.

Even homemade meals you prepare for your dog may not be as nourishing as commercial foods. The main drawback to do-it-yourself dog foods is that you can slave over a warm stove for hours and still not be positive that your dog's getting the full spectrum of nourishment he needs. Independent studies have worked out tables of various nutrients an average-sized dog requires, per pound of body weight. But such tables aren't of much practical use. Unless you're a professional chemist or sell health-food supplements for a living, where are you going to come by .072 milligrams of selenium, which is the daily ration for a thirty-pound dog? If you are cooking for your dog, it won't be easy to come up with a digestible, nutritious diet or to duplicate the full spectrum of nutrients available in a single serving of commercial dog food—and in the long run, we believe you're better off resorting to one of the so-called complete and balanced brands, supplemented with some of the extras outlined in Chapter 10.

Complex as it may seem, the science of nutrition addresses itself to only two basic questions: (1) What substances are present in any given food? and (2) What can the body do with those substances?

Let's start with the first question. Most nutritionists find it handy to divide all the substances you (or your dog) ingest into two main classes: *Macro*nutrients, those substances that the body requires in large quantities (namely, proteins, fats, and carbohydrates), and *micro*nutrients, vitamins and minerals that are equally important but required in far smaller amounts. Along with these nutrients, fiber is needed in the diet to help the body utilize these substances.

MACRONUTRIENTS

Carbohydrates

Carbohydrates are the closest things to an "instant" food for the body. Sugars (and, to a lesser degree, starches) are broken down quickly in the stomach, easily processed by the liver, and can get into the bloodstream within minutes of being eaten to provide needed energy. Glucose is the sugar that a mammal's body can use most directly. If it's not present in your dog's food, then his liver will convert other carbohydrates into glucose. Sucrose, or vegetable sugar, is nearly as efficient. Least useful of all is lactose, or milk sugar. After your dog leaves puppyhood, he may lose the ability to digest lactose at all, and milk can cause digestive upsets and diarrhea.

Animals cannot manufacture starches from scratch, as plants do, and they can store only limited amounts of animal starch, or glycerin. Your dog can't digest starches as effectively as you can; but dogs have survived for long periods on bread alone, and on diets consisting of up to 80 percent cereals—providing the rest of their diet is nourishing enough to keep their systems at peak health and efficiency. Studies have proven that the canine digestive tract can handle large quantities of starch, as long as it is first broken down by heat—in other words, cooked. Otherwise, your dog cannot digest them, and starches will pass right through your dog's system. It's true that cooking does destroy some of the vitamins and minerals in any food, but without this thermal predigestion, your dog won't be able to get much benefit.

Taken together, sugars and starches provide the fuel that your dog needs to keep his body running. If there aren't enough carbohydrates in his diet, his liver will go into action and synthesize the needed glucose from the other two groups of macronutrients.

Fats

Recent findings about human obesity and heart disease have given fat a bad name. Certainly it's not healthy for man or beast to be overweight. But the current spate of diet books and low-fat regimens tend to obscure the fact that any healthy diet *must* include a minimal amount of fatty acids. Moreover, next to glucose, stored fat is the body's favorite energy food. Fat is an *extremely* concentrated source of energy.

If an animal had to draw *all* its energy directly from food in the digestive tract, its blood-sugar level would plummet dangerously between meals, probably leading to coma and speedy death. A good amount of sugar and starch is stored in the liver, to be released as needed into the bloodstream. But in case the liver runs low, every mammal maintains a fairly substantial reserve of fat—right under the skin, where it also serves as insulation and as a protective layer for underlying tissues.

In short, then, a perfectly fit and healthy dog will still maintain a modest "bank account" of high-energy fat—even if you are feeding him a low-fat diet. But the fats an animal *eats* are not nearly as easy to metabolize or digest. Before the body can utilize them effectively, the fats must be broken down by special enzymes secreted by the liver and stored in the gall bladder. Therefore, if you feed your dog only the minimum fat he needs for good health, he'll find his meals easier to digest.

Proteins

There are twenty-two primary amino acids, or proteins. Your dog can manufacture twelve of them in sufficient quantities for his needs, but he has to get the remaining ten directly from his food. Ideally, a dog should use all these proteins for the maintenance, growth, and repair of body tissue rather than as a source of energy. But actually, at least 12 percent of the proteins consumed by an adult dog are burned for energy, even if he's being fed an adequate supply of carbohydrates and fats.

Use of such a small percentage of proteins for energy is fine. Problems can occur, however, if a dog isn't fed enough of the other two macronutrients—carbohydrates and fats—whose main job is to produce energy. When a dog dips into his protein rations in search of energy, he takes needed nutrients away from their main job. Protein metabolism puts a heavy strain on the liver—and when oxidized for energy, proteins produce large quantities of nitrogen compounds as by-products. These nitrogenous wastes are toxic in any quantity and so must be quickly excreted from the body, which puts a considerable strain on the kidneys. A long-term lack of carbohydrates in your dog's diet can upset his normal utilization of protein. Even before a dog's fat reserves are exhausted, the body may begin breaking down its own proteins—including those in the heart muscle!—to obtain energy. The animal needs to drink large amounts of water to help the kidneys flush away the toxic by-products—which is why animals can survive for several weeks without food, but only a few days without water.

It's helpful to think of all macro- and micronutrients as a form of currency. Fats, carbohydrates, and (to an extent) proteins are unrestricted funds—your dog's system can either "spend" them immediately for energy or "bank" them for later use.

MICRONUTRIENTS

Vitamins and Minerals

These elements and chemical compounds occur naturally, in varying amounts, in practically every foodstuff. In the body, many vitamins and minerals serve as catalysts, assisting in metabolic and digestive functions. others serve as building blocks of various tissues. For example, calcium is a major component of the teeth and skeletal system, and iron is a vital ingredient in the hemoglobin that allows red blood cells to absorb oxygen. A number of these micronutrients—particularly the fat-soluble vitamins like A, D, and E, and minerals like iron and calcium—can be "banked" in the liver or in body tissues. Should your dog's diet be briefly lacking in any one of these, he can always dip into his "account" to tide him over.

But it's not always healthy for him to do this. Whenever the system finds itself short of a given nutrient, its first move is to make a "withdrawal" from supplies already in the body. In the case of body fat, this is perfectly okay, because fat is stored *specifically* to be "withdrawn" later—and if your dog metabolizes a few ounces of fat, he'll be every bit as healthy as before. But problems arise when the body must draw from a stock of nutrients that are actively being *used* in other ways.

For example, if your dog isn't getting enough calcium in his food, he'll be forced to withdraw some from his skeletal system, which will make his bones and teeth a little bit weaker.

Then there are the "unbankables"—what scientists

refer to as *essential* nutrients. The body can't store or manufacture these substances on its own and must obtain them directly from the daily diet. For example, vitamin B_{12} and zinc are absorbed through the intestines and used immediately. The body has no way of recovering them from body tissues, so it's vital that all these essential "unbankables" be present in your dog's daily diet.

FIBER

One important component of a dog's diet that has nothing to do with nutrition but a lot to do with digestion is vegetable fiber. Science fiction writers have often speculated about a sort of super vitamin pill that, taken once a day, would supply all of the body's needs. but even such a pill would lack the one essential for any diet: bulk. A digestive system of any mammal, your dog's included, needs a certain amount of sheer roughage for the stomach and intestines to "get a grip on." If your dog's diet lacks fiber, you may find him eating grass. Sometimes dogs often vomit the grass up again, indicating that they have eaten it as an emetic. But other times they will pass the grass right on through in their feces—undigested, of course, but with no ill effects.

Experiments show that this kind of roughage stimulates a dog's intestines, giving the food a consistency that aids in later elimination. Chopped vegetables are better than grass for adding bulk to your dog's meals. But cooking them first will make them softer and gentler on your dog's innards; more important, cooking breaks down the cell walls so that important micronutrients can leach out.

THE NUTRITION PARADOX

Do we know how much of each nutrient your dog needs? Yes and no. On the one hand, most breeds of dogs digest and absorb nutrients in exactly the same way. Thus (with rare exceptions), what's good for a beagle will be equally good for a chow chow or a St. Bernard. And it's been fairly easy to determine a dog's basic requirements. Because of their relatively short life spans and early sexual maturity, dogs show the effects of any dietary deficiency more quickly than humans do—and within a mere five years, researchers can trace long-term nutritional lacks through as many as four generations of dogs. In one particular experiment, three generations of dogs were raised on a diet of beefsteak, rib roast, and hamburger. They grew and reproduced normally, but by the third generation, a high proportion of the puppies died before they could be weaned. Though the exact reason this happened is unknown, we speculate that the inadequate diet had caused rapid genetic anomalies. The dogs were fed only protein derived from lean muscle meat and were given no energy foods in the form of carbohydrates and possibly even fats. Therefore, they had to use protein for both energy and tissue building, and their bodies were deprived of essential building blocks. On this dietary regime the vital organs of the dogs gradually deteriorated, and a pattern of damaged organs became ingrained in the animals' genetic codes and developed into hereditarily transferable traits. Each generation became slightly weaker than the previous one. After just three generations, pups were born with a general weakness affecting some or all of the vital body organs.

Many had so many genetic abnormalities that they could not sustain life.

This illustrates one of the problems of trying to establish a "minimum" level of any given nutrient: an adequate diet is not necessarily a *healthy* diet. And in dogs too, not all dietary deficiencies produce immediate symptoms.

But what kind of diet does your dog need for best possible health? We don't know—simply because all of these nutritional studies have focused exclusively on deficiencies.

Folklore often emphasizes what an animal *can* do, as opposed to what the creature *should* do. For example, everyone's heard that goats will eat tin cans. They won't. Nor has any sane farmer tried to maintain his herd of goats on a scrap-metal diet! But a dog's infamous gulp-it-down, eat-anything-including-bones behavior has given rise to a similar myth—that dogs have cast-iron stomachs with digestive juices that rival a python's. And, sadly, this bit of "wisdom" is a leading cause of "misnourished" and undernourished pets.

It's true that a dog's stomach is so acidic that it can reduce bones to the consistency of rubber. But digestion is only half the battle. Because a dog can tolerate certain foods doesn't mean they are of any nutritional value to him. Only those nutrients that he absorbs from the digested foodstuff help him. The small intestine, where most absorption takes place, can handle only a limited range of proteins, fats, and carbohydrates.

A wide variety of foodstuffs is not the answer to a well-balanced diet. As many owners to their dismay have discovered, a sudden change in a dog's diet can "de-housebreak" him suddenly and swiftly. This occurs because an important final stage of your pet's digestion takes place in his large intestine. There a resident population of different strains of bacteria take over the job of breaking down the food—and, in the process, actually manufacture certain useful by-products, such as vitamin K and certain B vitamins. But each strain of bacteria is quite specific in what food substances it can handle. If you change his diet frequently, new strains of bacteria will have to multiply to cope with the new foodstuffs. At worst, your dog will suffer diarrhea. At best, he'll simply excrete the meal without deriving full benefit from it. Any nutrients his intestines don't absorb simply pass right on through, and, as one dog food manufacturer puts it, "The idea is to feed the dog, not the lawn."

You should feed your dog the same basic meal, day after day. But which food? What combination of macronutrients will produce the right micronutrients—the kinds the body can utilize to its best advantage? Not every nutrititional source is equal to every other nutritional source, nor is every mixture. Some micronutrients are broken down by the liver almost as soon as they're absorbed and then swiftly eliminated by the kidneys before they can do much good. Still others (certain amino acids, for example) are not used but are simply "banked" in the tissues, much as you might store spare parts in the trunk of your car. In terms of nutrition, protein is only as good as its weakest "unbankable" amino acid. That is, if one of the essential amino acids is at only half the level it should be, the body won't be able to use more than 50 percent of the other twenty-one amino acids, no matter how plentiful they may be. To be utilized properly, a protein must be *complete*—containing all the twenty-two amino acids, bankable and unbankable, in correct proportion to one another. This is true for minerals as well: phosphorus and calcium, for example, must be in a strict ratio for proper absorption. Micronutrients work *together* to nourish the body: except for certain "independents" like vitamin C and some of the B vitamins, most micronutrients must be present in given rations for the system to make good use of them.

A term often used by nutritionists is "biological value"—in other words, how well the body can make use of any given food. Recent studies have demonstrated that the protein found in vital organs is more easily digested than the protein found in lean meat, which probably explains why a wild dog begins by eating the internal organs of his prey, including the heart, liver, and lungs. One study ranked a number of common dog food components in terms of what percentage of their protein a dog can actually digest. Horsemeat leads the list at 91 percent. Next best are fish and liver meal (both at 88 percent), meat scraps and soybean meal (both at 86 percent), linseed meal (81 percent), and blood meal (71 percent).

It's no coincidence that foods with a high biological value are usually particularly rich in unbankable nutrients, because when it comes to many vitamins and minerals, a dog's absorption rates are even less efficient. For example, your pet can use better than half of the iron contained in heart, liver, and muscle tissue. But feed him blood meal, oysters, yeast, or cooked vegetables like alfalfa, oats, spinach, and wheat, and he won't be able to absorb more than one-quarter of the iron they contain.

Any one element can usually combine with a

number of others, and some of the resulting compounds are simply more absorbable than others. With copper, the efficiency is even less: only 5 percent of the copper in most foods is ever absorbed. But then, both iron and copper are bankable; copper is stored in the liver and iron in the mucous lining of the digestive tract, where they can be withdrawn as needed.

Your dog's ability to absorb given nutrients will vary throughout his lifetime. For example, puppies, pregnant bitches, and anemic adults all require extra iron, and they will assimilate iron more readily than normal. But certain physical abnormalities and degenerative diseases can impair the body's ability to process certain nutrients. Roundworms and other intestinal parasites can be responsible, as can problems with the pancreas and stomach. For example, gall bladder trouble or a liver ailment can cause bile to be secreted in less than normal quantities. This makes it hard for a dog to digest fats, which in turn slows his absorption of fat-soluble vitamins. In addition, unemulsified fats may adhere to food particles, forming an adhesive layer that effectively repels digestive enzymes, thus hampering your dog's absorption of *macro*nutrients as well.

Just to make things even trickier, your dog's nutrition can be thwarted by what some experts refer to as antivitamins, substances that block or inhibit the absorption of specific substances. A few antivitamins are biological red herrings, so chemically similar to the real things that the body gladly accepts them as substitutes, just as red blood cells will pick up carbon monoxide in preference to life-giving oxygen molecules. Mineral oil can absorb fat-soluble vitamins; so prolonged use of this (or, indeed, any form of laxative) can result in vitamin deficiencies.

Other antivitamins actively break down vitamins before they can reach the bloodstream. An enzyme common in raw fish quickly decomposes vitamin B_1, but, fortunately, this antivitamin is heat-sensitive and few dogs ingest raw fish. Possible exceptions are those dogs whose owners eat sashimi often and throw tidbits to their pets.

Most dogs should eat only once a day—so whatever concoction your pet eats has to contain everything he needs: the full spectrum of nutrients must appear in each meal. Therefore, every meal you serve your dog must contain all the necessary nutrients—macro- and micro-, bankable and unbankable; it must contain them in more than adequate amounts and in proper proportions to one another; and it must be an easily digestible preparation that provides just enough fiber to stimulate your dog's digestive system.

Every so often we get a call from a client who has just become a vegetarian and wants to know if his dog can share the regimen. It's certainly *possible* to keep a dog nourished and healthy on a no-meat diet, but it is a lot of work and requires a great deal of advance planning. Humans can easily obtain their daily protein ration from soybeans and dairy products. But dogs need five times more protein per pound of body weight than humans do. It's true that soybean meal and cornmeal are usually the main sources of protein in dry dog foods. Moreover, the proteins found in beans, barley, corn, and wheat are far more useful if they've been cooked, in which case their utilization rate jumps to between 75 and 94 percent. But the fact remains that your dog's system isn't equipped to handle most vegetable proteins as effectively as yours is. As we've already explained, horsemeat and organ meats have the greatest biological value.

Even a vegetarian dog shouldn't be given only vegetables. Some experts estimate that because of cooked vegetables' potential laxative effect, they should constitute no more than 25 percent of a dog's total diet. More than that can force the digestive tract to work overtime (and, as we'll explain in the next chapter, move food through the body too swiftly for proper absorption of nutrients). And lastly, there's simply no vegetarian substitute for the fatty acids your dog needs to maintain a shiny, glossy coat. He'll probably be better off if you don't insist that he share your eating preference.

3

The Four Basic Types of Commercial Dog Food

The type—not brand—of food you feed your dog is probably the single most important factor in shaping his health and behavior. When you go shopping, you have four basic choices—canned, semimoist, dry, and self-proclaimed professional dog foods. Ironically, these four different types came into being not because of any new discoveries about canine nutrition but in response to the buying habits of the American consumer.

CANNED WORKS

In the days before World War II, most dogs were still being fed table scraps plus other kitchen discards. This was convenient because, back in the days before supermarkets, a dog owner could stop at the local butcher and get all sorts of bones, trimmings, and other odds and ends for Fido, often at no expense at all. (One can still do this in Europe and, especially, in many countries throughout Latin America.) According to some present-day experts, this feeding often resulted in a "haphazard" diet.

In the 1950s, canned dog food—the original form of commercial dog food—appeared in stores. It was marketed principally as a time-saver; no longer did dog owners have to make special trips to the butcher or sort out palatable tidbits from the kitchen. Even better, canned-food buyers were assured that their pets were getting the proper nourishment in the proper amounts. Most canned meats consisted of horsemeat or beef muscle, together with varying amounts of poultry, fish, and "meat by-products"—those highly nutritious stomachs, lips, udders, and smooth gastrointestinal-muscle discards that no butcher shop would ever see. The best canned dog foods were supplemented with vitamins and minerals to replace micronutrients that had been destroyed during cooking and storage. And, as a side benefit, the family pet was less likely to suffer an upset stomach or diarrhea from rich, spicy leftovers.

Canned dog food caught on in a big way. But until the 1960s, sales were still relatively modest. Then, as Thomas Whiteside noted in *The New Yorker*, the United States' pet population had a sudden baby boom of its own, increasing by about 50 percent in the decade between 1964 and 1974. In that same period, however, pet food sales increased by a whopping 250 percent. By 1976, they had reached an astounding $2.5 billion annually, outselling commercially prepared baby foods by more than 3 to 1. Of course, most dogs eat more than most babies—a canine weighing around 65 pounds can consume at least 500 pounds of dog food a year. But this staggering increase was all largely thanks to a number of highly aggressive advertising campaigns.

In addition, we believe, American consumers had gotten used to concentrated fruit juices, dehydrated fruit, cake mixes, instant coffee, instant oatmeal—all of which can be prepared for eating if you "just add water." In other words, consumers had been taught to see watery products as a waste of money; and in canned dog foods, water accounts for about 75 percent of the contents, by weight.

The times—and the market—were ripe for dry food. Cattle had been doing fine for years on dry milled feed, and it didn't cost much to adapt the same technique to process quantities of high-protein fish meal and grain into a food for dogs. From a consumer point of view, dry food was the ultimate in aesthetics—with no odor and no greasy wetness, it was as far removed from a carcass as you could possibly get. Because most of its moisture had been evaporated, it had many of the virtues of the popular "instant" mixes, including convenience and a long shelf life. And, of course, dry food was inexpensive, since dry weight allows for lower shipping costs and cheaper, non-waterproof packaging. Customers could buy fifty-pound economy sacks for even greater savings.

The dry food had other advantages. The crunchy texture, many manufacturers claimed, was good for the animal's teeth. And dry dog food wouldn't spoil if left in the bowl. Therefore, puppies could be taught to "self-feed"—to take short meals throughout the day from a bowl kept constantly full. This meant much greater convenience for owners, plus the satisfaction of knowing that the dogs were somehow becoming responsible for their own feeding, just like *real* family members. Dry foods started out second to cans, but, by the mid-1970s, had pulled ahead and were generating far greater dollar volume.

THE DRY DILEMMA

Creating a brand-new kind of dog food is really an awesome responsibility. The manufacturer has to assume that its product will be the *only* food the dog ever eats; and most self-respecting companies take pains to run extensive nutritional studies with a new product, which means following dogs through several generations to see if any deficiencies, long-term or otherwise, crop up. So it was with dry dog food, but for one problem—virtually all the research took place in kennels and laboratories, where dogs were confined and not able to get into trouble. The studies concentrated on concrete, measurable factors, such as muscle tone, appearance of skin and hair, growth rate, alertness, and reproductive capability. (As we'll explain, canine malnutrition has a drastic effect on fertility.) But little or no attention was paid to these animals' *behavior*. A lovable pet is more than just a package of healthy organs wrapped in a sleek fur coat. And any dog food research that doesn't take behavior and trainability into account is apt to shortchange the owner.

Dry foods, basically, are mixtures of flakes and powders made by blending cooked cereals with other high-protein, easy-to-digest products like dry milk, meat meal and fish meal, plus vitamins and mineral supplements. Whether the manufacturer says the dry food is roasted, baked, or air blown, it's essentially a dehydrated food or, as the experts say, "extruded," and thus similar to our own breakfast cereals. But how often do you like to eat a bowl of cornflakes without milk or shredded wheat straight from the box?

Perhaps the best way to dramatize the point we're going to make is to compare the actual moisture content of dog food with that of foods that commonly appear on the human dinner table. By weight, most vegetables contain between 75 and 95 percent water. Meats range from 50 to 75 percent water—a nice juicy sirloin steak is approximately three-quarters H_2O, which is the same as canned dog food. But dry dog food contains only 7 to 10 percent water. (Although totally dry when it leaves the plant, any dry food will reabsorb a certain amount of moisture from the air.) This percentage compares with dry cereal (10 percent), dry flour (10 to 12 percent), and dry roasted nuts (5 to 8 percent).

As you've already learned, a dog instinctively eats until his stomach is full, and then some. This means that when fed dry food, within a few minutes, your dog will fill his stomach with food that's been moistened only slightly by his saliva and gastric juices. Now, as any bartender who serves free nuts and pretzels will proudly attest, the more dry foods you consume, the greater your thirst and the more you'll drink. Any dehydrated or naturally dry food must absorb moisture before digestive enzymes can handle it. Porous dog food, moreover, operates like a sponge, absorbing water from elsewhere in the digestive tract and creating a potentially serious imbalance.

So what does your dog do? Feeling thirsty, he crosses over to his water dish and starts drinking—in hearty gulps. And this is where the trouble begins. The dry food expands significantly as it absorbs water. And that expansion process begins inside your dog's, already full stomach! Of course you can soak dry food in water before feeding your pet, but that solution isn't as simple as you might think. A chemist friend of ours performed some experiments on dry dog food for us. After soaking one cup of dry food in pure water for two hours, she discovered that the food absorbed a total of one cup of liquid. (Since dry food comes in chunks, and a cupful of it contains a certain amount of empty air, this suggests that dry food absorbs more than its volume in water.) But this experiment, we suspected, wasn't wholly accurate in simulating what occurs in a dog's stomach, because canine gastric juices contain a high concentration of hydrochloric acid. In a sense, this acid takes the place of chewing and breaks down foodstuffs so that they present the greatest possible surface area.

As the chemist explained it, acidity is measured by pH—a number that refers to the number of hydrogen ions in any given substance. The pH scale runs from 1 (the most acid) to 14 (the most alkaline), with a pH of 7 being about neutral. Human stomach acids have a pH of around 2, though the moisture present in the foods we eat dilutes this to a pH of 3 or 4. Your pet's undiluted acid is even stronger. If he's ever swallowed chunks of rawhide chew-toys, you'll know that he can digest them very nicely. Indeed, laboratory studies prove that bone fragments that no human could digest become soft and pliable in less than an hour after being soaked in a dog's stomach acid. This result doesn't mean you can ignore the warning not to feed your dog bones that can splinter, because bone fragments can pierce the lining of your dog's intestinal tract and cause severe damage. These studies were designed only to show the strength of your dog's digestive juices.

Would the low pH of a dog's gastric juices affect the quantity of water that dry dog food absorbs? At our request, the chemist soaked a second cup of dry food in water to which she had added mildly acidic white vinegar. To our surprise, the food absorbed one and a quarter cups of this solution. This suggests that even if you do presoak dry food, it's likely to expand even further in the presence of your dog's gastric juices, which are far more acidic than the white vinegar used in our test.

In practical terms, this makes it hard to judge the proper quantity of dry food by sight alone. You may think you're serving your dog a reasonable amount by allowing him only three-quarters of a bowl of dry kibble. But after that dry measure has absorbed water, its bulk can increase by at least 125 percent.

You know how overeating makes *you* feel—gorged, heavy, and uncomfortable. The expansion of food in your dog's stomach produces an even more uncomfortable bloated feeling. This discomfort—occurring from one to two hours after he's lapped up the extra water—makes him restless and he'll seek to distract himself. A nervous dog will use his teeth much as humans fidget with their hands; thus his intestinal distress translates into an almost irresistible compulsion to chew.

Many dry food manufacturers claim that their products' crunchy, abrasive texture will help clean your dog's teeth. But this isn't the case. As you can observe, a dog crushes dry food only briefly on his back molars before gulping it down. If a dog fed on dry food displays clean teeth, it's probably because of the *other* things he's *driven* to chew on; and thus whatever you may have saved by buying dry food is spent for repairs to your rugs and furniture. Your dog's chewing on a piece of wood in the wild to keep his teeth clean is fine. But in your home, a chair or table leg is not a good substitute. You do have to keep your domestic dog's teeth clean, and in Chapter 11 we tell you how—only a toothbrush will remove accumulated tartar.

But there's a second, more insidious, side effect to dry dog food. As you know, a dog's digestive tract is equipped to handle large quantities of food—but to do so, it must shift into high gear, moving the gorged food rapidly onward to make extra room in the stomach. A dog's small intestine, though, is so short that food passing through too quickly may not give up all its nutrients, or may even not be completely digested. Here, then, is yet another paradox of canine digestion: overfeeding can actually contribute to malnutrition.

The latest addition to the dry foods parade is what the manufacturers call "high density" food. Again, this was introduced to overcome some of the prejudices and objections that consumers were voicing about dry dog foods in general—mainly that they weren't nutritious enough. High-density foods supposedly are manufactured by a "special" baking process that doesn't puff the food up with so much air; the dog is supposed to derive more nourishment per volume of food he eats.

Of course, this "improvement" in processing justifies a slightly higher price. But the fallacy in the argument is that your dog is still getting the same amount of nutrition per *weight*. Sure, he may be able to swallow more of a densely packed food, but it will expand just as much with water as does its puffier equivalent. Dense food, though, may not absorb water as thoroughly or as rapidly, and one manufacturer actually claims that high-density food passes through a dog's system without absorbing too much water. And this can lead to severe constipation (see Chapter 7). All in all, high-density foods are probably less digestible than the ordinary dry variety.

We would prefer you not use dry food. But dry food is an economic necessity for many people. Therefore, if you must use dry food, be sure to presoak it and make sure it's expanded to its maximum bulk in the bowl *before* your dog eats it. Mix one and one-half to two cups of water with every cup of dry food you feed your dog. Place the bowl on your kitchen counter and let it sit for an hour or so until the food is thoroughly soaked. When it's ready, feed this mixture to your dog, leaving excess water as gravy. (Nutrients may have leached out into the water, and if you drain it off, you could be depriving your pet of nutritional requirements.)

THE SEMIMOIST "BURGER" FOODS

Meanwhile, back on Madison Avenue, market researchers discovered that many owners were feeling guilty about feeding their dogs dry dog food, if only because it was so far removed from those meaty, tangy, flavorful canned brands that were advertising themselves on TV. Their response was a semimoist patty wrapped in plastic, which bore a close resemblance to fresh hamburger yet offered most of the conveniences of dry foods. A mixture of beef and beef by-products with a balanced supplement of fats, vitamins, and minerals, semimoist foods were at least 95 percent digestible, according to one university study. Also, they were cosmetically attractive, with no strong odor perceptible to humans though dogs seemed to like the smell. And they certainly were easy to serve—just rip open the individual cellophane packet and drop the pre-measured patty into the dog's dish, without even touching it. There were no bulky cans to throw away, no spoons to clean. One semimoist manufacturer referred to its product as "the canned dog food without the can."

When semimoist foods were about to go on the shelves, we were hired to train the canine actors for one of the first commercials. The script called for the dogs to choose the new semimoist product over ordinary hamburger—and according to Federal Communications Commission guidelines, the test couldn't be faked. To be sure the semimoist patties would come out ahead, we placed them and the hamburger in a refrigerator (by storing both foods under identical conditions, we were within the FCC guidelines) until it was time to shoot the commercial. By then, the hamburger was quite cold and, because low temperatures inhibit odor, relatively unappealing to the canine noses. But even under refrigeration, the semimoist patties retained whatever aroma they already had—and this technique we thought up based on our knowledge of a dog's sense of smell induced the dogs to select the semimoist food on camera.

The commercial was a great success, and along with

our salary the manufacturer threw in a bonus: a free supply of semimoist food for our four dogs. For a while we were convinced that this product was a real break-through in dog food—especially since Snap, Inches, Plum, and Sleepy all obviously loved it. In addition, the dogs' stools were firm and reddish brown. This may seem like a bizarre benefit, but the appearance of a dog's feces is often touted as an important clue to his general health and the digestibility of his diet. In fact, one manufacturer actually claims that semimoist foods "are more dependable than canned foods for produc-ing firm, soft [sic] feces considered indicative of good health." But like so many other convenience-oriented wonders, semimoist food let us down.

As our dogs continued on their diet of semimoist patties, we noticed that they started drinking more water than before. We didn't realize exactly why until one day when we accidentally spilled some water into Plum's food bowl. The semimoist patty turned pale and began to expand. In other words, the patty didn't con-tain enough natural moisture, and our dogs were drink-ing more to compensate. (Semimoist patties, containing about 36 percent water, are comparable to bread with 36 percent and cheddar cheese at between 35 and 50 percent.) It was also likely that the semimoist fare would expand slightly in a dog's stomach. On further investigation, we discovered that semimoist was also high in salt and preservatives. (After all, it was engineered to be stored at room temperature.) Worse still, it contained quantities of sugar, with up to 25 percent sucrose in the form of sugar beets (sugar canes also contain sucrose)—a shortcoming that many can-ned dog food manufacturers later pointed to in advertisements trying to recapture their share of the market.

After we put our dogs back on a canned food regimen, they promptly cut down on their water intake. After a few weeks, Plum's coat became noticeably more shiny—a surprise to us, because we hadn't noticed the gradual dulling that must have occurred while he was on a diet of semimoist food. (We didn't notice the same change in our Maltese spaniels simply because such alterations show up more dramatically in a short-haired dog.) Their stools changed only in that they were less dry in texture. We had been worried that the "perfect stool" side benefit claimed by the manufacturer of semimoist food would disappear once we stopped the food. It didn't.

Now there was only one puzzle left: Why had our dogs enjoyed the semimoist food so much? Then we remembered our commercial, and how the refrigerated patties still smelled good to our canine actors. Though *we* couldn't detect any distinctive odor to the semimoist food, the manufacturers' chemists must have found it simple to add some ingredient that appeals to a dog's extraordinarily sensitive nose.

This brings up another problem with commercial foods in general. When a company introduces additives, it's not always for nutritional reasons. Since a dog is genetically programmed to eat as much as he can, he'll most likely polish off any food that's put in front of him, particularly if he's fed only once a day. Most owners, however, get their dogs as puppies when their stomachs are still fairly small. When the puppy doesn't finish his meal, the owner seldom realizes that it's because he simply can't hold that much; and then the owner blames the dog food company. As one advertising survey noted, "Foods the dog rejects or . . . eats reluctantly will not be repurchased." On top of that, as we'll explain in the next chapter, adult dogs can quickly learn to become finicky eaters. Consequently, there is an ongoing corporate search for extra ingredients that dogs find irresistible, quite apart from any nutritional benefit.

Such taste-appeal is trickier to achieve than you might think, because you can determine a dog's preferences only through behavior. All an observer can ask, really, is whether the dog prefers A or B—as we discovered in filming that semimoist commercial. It's no trade secret that dogs like the "meaty" smell of fats and proteins or that cheese and egg flavors score high with both cats and dogs. But, essentially, all such testing is basically trial and error, and when the difference between two foods narrows too much, the test animals may no longer bother to discriminate between them.

When in doubt, it's always cheaper to "improve" flavor by simply adding sugar and salt, both of which semimoist patties offer in abundance. After all, if a dog wolfs down his meal and begs for more, what kind owner isn't going to increase his ration by just one more patty? Increased consumption means quicker sales, and higher profits. But refined sugar is not perfectly digestible, since many of the natural enzymes that assist in its breakdown are removed during the refining process. In order to make refined sugar, sucrose from sugarcane and beets is stripped of many of its natural components and turned into granular form. (Because it has many contaminants, pure, unrefined sugar is illegal in the United States.) Once refined, sugar has no nutritional benefits. Plus, if your dog's diet is too rich in sugar, his pancreas must work overtime to secrete enough insulin to stabilize his blood sugar level—and, at the very best, sugars not burned for energy will be converted into body fat.

The semimoist's high salt content stimulates your dog's thirst, further increasing his desire for water. It's certainly the most highly processed of the three kinds of dog food discussed thus far and lacks most of the bulk present in the other two. Also, semimoists get most of their consistency from corn syrup, which is not particularly good for a dog's teeth.

As should now be abundantly clear, how quickly your dog takes to any given food has little to do with how nourishing it is. Biological value rarely correlates with whether it smells good to you or is easy to serve. In our opinion, semimoist and dry foods are more like fuel for a machine than food for a dog.

THE SO-CALLED PROFESSIONAL FOODS

For years, many restaurant owners have known that for customers willing to pay a premium for gourmet fare, part of the reason is snob appeal. After all, isn't this the kind of cuisine enjoyed by royalty and socialites? Similarly, what dog owner isn't tempted to give his pet a "breakfast of champions"—the diet allegedly fed to world-class show dogs and pedigreed breeding stock? Now there are four grades of ready-made dog food— the three commercial types we've just been discussing plus *professional* dog food, which claims to be of vastly higher quality and is demonstrably more expensive. In fact, it's easiest to distinguish professional dog foods by their high prices, relatively new brand names, and advertisements stating that they are better prepared—and, by implication, more nourishing—than anything you could buy in a supermarket.

A good part of this advertising appeals to elitists. One professional blend, for example, says that it "is not the food for every dog, or for that matter, every kennel. [Our brand] has been developed for, and is being made available to, *only those kennels with the highest standards in the dog* industry. . . . [Our brand] is for working and show animals where *only the highest standards can be appreciated.* [Emphasis added.] Therefore, we do not recommend the purchase of this unique food if the results you currently get from your feeding program are satisfactory." So, there! Significantly, though, this brand uses the same "Your dog's gonna love it" pitch that the commercial brands employ: "Method of feeding: Pour in a dish and stand aside!"

On the plus side, professional foods often dispense with synthetic sweeteners, colorings, flavors, sugar, and other additives. But the "healthy" ingredients that professional foods do include are of dubious value.

On the principle that dog owners like to feed their pets the same foods they eat themselves, some dog food manufacturers are now pushing health diets for dogs. Often such health and professional diets are simply too rich for a sedentary dog and contain an imbalance of necessary ingredients. Remember, too, that the high price of these foods may reflect nothing more than a low sales volume. One manufacturer of "high-quality" dog food admitted to us that he had to settle for marketing a product that offered "the maximum quality for the minimum cost." But a larger company, with greater buying power, might well be able to purchase better ingredients at lower prices.

Certainly there are significant differences in the composition of various professional foods, but it's hard to tell how meaningful they are without a breakdown of their micronutrient content. In short, we believe that *most* canned dog foods are better than dry or semi-moist foods. Of the three mass-produced commercial foods available, canned foods most closely approximate the materials a dog is naturally able to digest—that is, meats, cooked vegetables, and cooked grain products. Also the least processed of the three kinds, canned foods contain a proper percentage of moisture as well as efficient, whole proteins in the form of organ meats, fish, or eggs—though, naturally, the quality, source, and amounts of these proteins vary according to brand.

LABEL AND PRESERVATIVE RUBRICS

To figure out exactly what's inside, read the label. In this country, any dog food marked "complete and balanced" must be able to fulfill all of an animal's normal nutritional needs. (This law doesn't apply, of course, to foods manufactured for sale outside the U.S.) As for contents, labels are usually useful, though not explicit. If you pick up a can labeled chicken, for example, by law it must contain *only* chicken as its main ingredient, though other meats or meat by-products may be added as fillers. But exactly what does "meat and meat by-products" stand for? At the Department of Agriculture, the by-products used for dog food are termed "4D meat," which comes from disabled, dying, diseased, or dead animals, and thus they are not fit for human consumption. But there's no chance of infecting or poisoning your dog; all such meats are processed at temperatures high enough to kill disease organisms and break down bacterial toxins. And, even after the processing, these innards are still more nourishing than ordinary lean meat.

You might assume that the more ingredients listed on the label, the more the manufacturer is giving you credit for being intelligent and well-informed. However, all too many dog foods are enriched or improved with what can only be called marketing power—attractive packaging and advertising claims that do little or nothing for your dog's nutrition.

A guarantee that your dog will like the food probably means that the flavor's been enhanced by additives. Therefore, you should skip such products and also look for ones with as few preservatives as possible. Anything added to "retard spoilage" is a preservative. In semimoist foods at least, the chief chemical used is PCC propylene glycol—chemically similar to embalming fluid and antifreeze. But when you open a can of preservative-free dog food, give the contents a quick whiff to make sure it hasn't turned rancid.

Furthermore, you have to consider the preservatives that give dry dog food its long shelf life. Many artificial preservatives have been shown to cause cancer in laboratory animals. (After all, preservatives are nothing more than substances toxic to bacteria—and if they're no good for one-celled organisms, why should they be friendly to higher forms of life?) In response to consumer concern, many manufacturers have started using vitamin C instead—the artificial ascorbic acid, which is not as nourishing as the C derived from organic sources. According to one manufacturer's claim, a sealed bag of dry dog food with ascorbic preservatives has a shelf life of one year. Even so, be sure to check the expiration date on the bag and to buy the latest date you can find. And never leave dry food, soaked or unsoaked, in your dog's bowl for more than two hours.

As we'll explain in the next chapter, it's best to stick with a brand you find nutritious *and* palatable to your dog. Don't keep switching brands. Save labels from the cans, so that you can tell when a company changes the proportions of ingredients or adds new ones.

Then, what if your favorite brand suddenly blooms with additives and multisyllabic chemicals? Or if the contents—formerly helpful and detailed—suddenly become incomprehensible? There is something you can do! The very best way to keep dog food manufacturers honest and responsive to your pet's needs is to write a letter, preferably to the president or chairman of the board. Complain, and state your feelings! Many people believe a letter from a single individual is ignored, but that's not so. As one corporate spokesman told us (after we promised we wouldn't use his name), "You wouldn't believe the clout a single letter carries! So few people bother to write at all that whenever someone does, the president starts worrying how many other people out there feel the same way. Even if that particular letter never gets answered, we treat it as the voice of maybe a thousand, two thousand people who didn't take the trouble to complain."

4

The Five Stages of Canine Feeding Schedules

 Dog owners are often so busy that they'll gladly adopt any feeding schedule that promises them the most convenience. And certainly the most effortless method of all is the so-called self-feeding technique. Not that the dog's expected to open a can for himself; instead, dry or semimoist food is constantly available in his bowl, twenty-four hours a day.

The brochure put out by one dog food manufacturer asserts that this "practice is gaining in popularity among breeders and individual dog owners. . . . The puppy or dog . . . can eat as much or as little as he wants to, whenever he wants to." This, of course, keeps guilty owners from having to worry about whether they'll get home in time to feed their hungry pets. Self-feeding, the brochure adds, "eliminates boredom" in dogs and thus reduces their tendency to chew on rugs and furniture.

At first glance, this system does seem sensible.

Rather than loading the dog's stomach with one big quick-expanding meal a day, doesn't it make sense to let him nibble small snacks whenever he feels like it? Unfortunately, no!

Here is a classic example of how self-feeding can go wrong. One of our clients called us because her full-grown standard poodle was no longer sleeping at the foot of her bed, as he'd been doing since he was a puppy. Rather, the dog was awakening at night and roaming through the apartment. His owner, wondering what was bothering him, kept getting up to make sure all her doors and windows were locked—and soon started losing sleep herself. Finally, after she found herself only half awake at the office one day, she gave us a call. We soon discovered that despite this woman's heavy schedule, she still managed to take her poodle out for a run in the early morning and again in the early evening. In between, she provided the dog with a constant supply of semimoist food on the assumption that he would eat gradually, all day long. But no dog likes to exercise on a full stomach. Therefore, the poodle would deliberately eat sparingly during the afternoon in anticipation of his evening romp. Then, about an hour or two after working up a good appetite, he would polish off everything left in his bowl. And at night, that extra load of semimoist, semi-expandable, salty, sugary food was still weighing on his stomach, making him sleepless and uncomfortable. When his owner switched him to *one* meal of canned food in the evening right after his exercise, his hungry stomach had plenty of time to digest it before they both turned in—and so he went back to sleeping comfortably at the foot of her bed.

It's no surprise that the dry and semimoist manufacturers should advocate self-feeding. Since canned dog food quickly spoils after a few hours at room temperature, self-feeding more or less forces you to rely on one of the other two kinds. And if your dog is deciding his own mealtimes and portions, he's likely to wind up eating more—which, naturally, translates into your buying more.

If you read self-feeding brochures, it becomes clear where the idea originated: "*In a kennel,* [self-feeding] has a quieting effect on the dogs, and there is no before-mealtime nervous excitement. Being able to nibble at will not only gives the dogs something to do and prevents boredom, but generally prevents the habit of coprophagy [eating of feces]. . . . Self-feeding has a distinct advantage because the less aggressive animals are able to get their share. 'Poor doers' *in a kennel* generally respond to a self-feeding program. [Emphasis added.]"

In other words, self-feeding was developed for, and can be beneficial to, dogs confined in kennels. These animals may well be loved and kept in good care, but dogs confined within a cage or enclosure don't need to be as well-behaved as the pet in your home or apartment.

We believe that one of the major steps to a well behaved dog is to have him on a regular feeding schedule. Your dog has to learn to live within the confines of your life-style. Feeding your dog at regular times convenient for you is a major step toward a trained dog. An important tenet in using food to control your dog's behavior and health is also a physiological fact; your dog's digestive system needs to rest between meals.

YOUR DOG'S DIGESTIVE DEVELOPMENT

As he matures, from conception through young adulthood, your dog's digestive system evolves through five distinct stages, adapting itself to longer and longer intervals between meals.

Stage One

A developing embryo receives a twenty-four-hour-a-day bath of nutrients drawn from the mother's bloodstream. During the latter stages of fetal development, when the digestive tract is fully formed, the unborn puppy swallows amniotic fluid, giving his intestines and kidneys a chance to practice handling liquids.

Stage Two

Shortly after birth, a puppy begins to use his digestive system for the first time to obtain nutrients. Within hours, each newborn puppy chooses a nipple to which he will return for subsequent feedings. It's crucial that puppies nurse during their first twenty-four hours of life because the mother's first milk (colostrum) is exceptionally rich in vitamins, fats, and protein, as well as antibodies that give the puppies temporary protection against whatever diseases their mother is immune. But a mother dog doesn't nurse her litter whenever they want. It's *her* choice as to when the pups get to suckle, and her schedule in turn is dictated by the fullness of milk in her teats. So even from birth, puppies are on a schedule of sorts.

Stage Three

The weaning period, during which time the puppy's digestive tract slowly gains the strength to handle solid foods, is an important time. A mother dog will usually wean her litter by regurgitating her own food for them to eat. Since this food is already partly digested, the pups can handle it with little trouble. Finally, the mother's milk dries up—whether naturally or with the help of a veterinarian's medicine—and the six-week-old puppy is ready to leave his mother.

Stage Four

This usually occurs when a new dog enters your home. He's been eating solid food for less than a month now, and his digestive tract is still not as totally efficient as it'll be in a few months. So you must make allowances for his weak stomach—and for his growing body, as well. Paradoxically, though the dog's growth rate is slowing, he's putting on more weight in actual pounds, so his nutrition needs are about double that of an adult dog of the same size.

By this time, the breeder or pet shop owner should have taught the puppy to eat from a bowl. When you get him home, start your new puppy off with one of the canned dog foods formulated especially for puppies. Mix in enough water to make a semisolid gruel. If you have more than one puppy, make sure each one has his own dish. Some experts advise you not to worry about competition: a puppy who has a bowl all to himself will grow up to be a fussy eater. In our experience, feeding more than one dog from the same bowl only encourages fighting and makes it virtually impossible to tell if each puppy is getting his fair share. (For more on establishing proper eating habits, see Chapter 7.)

After a full year of growth, most breeds of dogs will have multiplied their birth weight by fifty times—and most of this spurt occurs before the age of six months. Your puppy, then, needs to eat more than an adult dog of the same weight, but there's no way his stomach can hold all that bulk at a single sitting. Therefore, the best schedule for a new puppy is three meals a day—morning, noon, and late afternoon. This will put minimal strain on his still-growing digestive tract and ensure that he's getting maximum benefit from what he consumes. Some experts recommend feeding a puppy even more frequently at this age. But why make it any harder for him to learn the rules of housebreaking? As we'll explain in Chapter 6, a dog learns bowel and bladder control much faster without the added obstacle of an overworked digestive tract.

Unfortunately, many people who work from 9:00 to 5:00 can't make it home for a midday meal. But this should *not* be an excuse for self-feeding, because a puppy must be given no more than he can digest. Your puppy will get by just fine on two meals a day, as long as those meals are of very high biological value.

During these early months of a puppy's existence, excellent nutrition is absolutely crucial, since any deficiency can have serious results. Therefore, it makes good sense to fortify whatever food you're feeding your puppy with a vitamin supplement. Remember, too, that a growing dog needs about twice the calories of an adult dog of the same weight.

Some puppies will take their time eating; others

(especially if they had to contend with other dogs at the breeder's or pet shop) will bolt it down. A younger puppy may bolt his food rapidly, regurgitate it almost immediately, then return to it a few minutes later. This is entirely normal behavior, especially in just-weaned puppies who are not fully accustomed to solid food. The vomited fare is partly digested with enzymes and hydrochloric acid and thus gives the immature stomach a chance to try again.

In any case, a puppy should be done with his meal within a half hour's time. Once in a while, a dog who's teething may be reluctant to eat, and once in a while, dogs will skip a meal for reasons all their own. That's no cause for alarm; just remove the unwanted food and serve fresh food at the next regular mealtime. Do *not* pamper or bribe a reluctant puppy with treats from the table, or you'll be starting him on a lifetime career of begging—and possible malnutrition.

If every dog has his own bowl, you can see at a glance how much he's eating—or not eating, as the case may be. If he leaves food in the bowl, throw it out and feed him 20 percent less at his next meal. On the other hand, if he polishes off his entire dish and still looks hungry, increase his rations by 10 to 20 percent the next time. Up to around age four months, a dog needs to eat about one-eighth of his own body weight every day, which means there's not too much danger of his becoming too fat. The food should still be fairly moist and soupy, but with added *water,* not milk—at this stage of life, your puppy's digestive tract is losing its ability to handle lactose.

Regular feedings mean less likelihood of wasted food and digestive upsets, of which even healthy puppies have their fair share. Arrange it so the morning meal is lighter and the evening meal the heaviest—a pattern you can continue as the puppy gets older, until he's eating his entire ration at the end of the day. But don't skimp on the *total* volume you feed a growing puppy; in other words, alter the proportions, but not the amount.

A dog experiences a spurt of development during adolescence, from about five to seven months up to the time a female has her first heat and a male lifts his leg to urinate. But you can safely decrease the quantity of food so that, by nine months, your dog is getting only 25 percent more than his ordinary adult ration, together with any of the supplements covered in Chapter 10. Remember that larger breeds are slower to mature and may need extra food a bit longer than small breeds. But in any case, your dog can get by on an adult feeding schedule when he's still only six months old.

Stage Five

At this point, for all intents and purposes, your dog is in adulthood. By now, the "work" of growth and puberty are largely completed and your dog needs fewer micronutrients (and basically fewer calories) in the simple day-to-day maintenance of his body. After a dog is nine months old, he should definitely be on an adult regimen: a single meal in the late afternoon or early evening.

It's also a good idea, especially for the dog who has come to expect a morning feeding, to offer him one or two dog biscuits in the morning. The biscuits help settle his stomach and provide a bit of quick energy later in the day. Like most cookies and crackers for human consumption, dog biscuits are baked products made from a dough of soy or wheat flour and milk or milk products. All are rich in carbohydrates, and the best have added vitamins and minerals. Many of them, however, have additives and contain mere "empty calories" with little real nutrition, and you may find it convenient and rewarding to bake your own dog biscuits.

- Frances Sheridan Goulart gives this recipe for "Muttrecal Cookies" in her book *Bone Appetit:* Mix 1 cup of sprouted soybeans with a few drops of soy sauce, 1 tablespoon of vegetable oil, and a dash of sea salt. Spread the mixture in a thin layer on a greased cookie sheet and bake for 25 minutes at 325 degrees. Small fragments can be given as a treat or as breakfast. These biscuits are rich in protein and—with only 25 calories per tablespoon—hardly fattening. But for older dogs you may want to omit the soy sauce, which packs quite a wallop of salt.

- These liver biscuits were once used as rewards for dogs in obedience trials: Cut 1 pound of liver (any kind—calf, beef, pork) into small chunks, place them in a food processor, and blend until smooth. In a bowl mix this with 1½ cups of flour and 1 cup of cornmeal. Add 1 teaspoon of minced garlic or onion (for flavor) and bake on a greased cookie sheet for 20 minutes at 350°. Then cut into individual servings which can be frozen or refrigerated.

- The Westwood Friendship Lioness Club of Denver has invented a slightly more complex recipe for

"Good-Enough-for-Humans Dog Biscuits." Mix 2 packets of dry yeast in ½ cup of warm water. Add 4 cups of beef bouillon and mix. Then stir in 7 cups of white flour, 4 cups each of whole wheat flour, wheat germ, and cracked wheat; 2 cups each of cornmeal, oatmeal, and rye flour; 1 cup of dry milk, 2 teaspoons of onion or garlic salt, and 2 teaspoons of salt. Beat in a dozen eggs, knead thoroughly, roll out on a quarter-inch sheet, and cut to desired size. Bake on greased cookie sheets at 300°. After 45 minutes, turn off the oven and let the cookies cool and harden for at least 6 hours before removing them.

These three recipes have the advantages of containing no preservatives, being relatively sugar-free, and being much fresher than any biscuits you could buy in the store. As with other supplements discussed in Chapter 10, they can be used alongside commercial biscuits or as substitutes. But don't let your dog's enthusiasm for your cooking prompt you into giving him too many of them in any one day.

THE UNDERFEEDING STRATEGY

In a household with several dogs of different ages, it may not be practical to schedule more than one feeding time a day; it's not really fair to entice an older dog with the aroma of food he can't share. Happily, it's all right to rush things a bit and put a younger dog on an adult schedule a few months earlier than you might otherwise. Our first dog, Plum, had three meals a day until he was six months, two meals a day until he was a year old, and one meal a day thereafter. Inches, our first Maltese, thrived on only two meals a day until he was six months old, when we switched him to Plum's adult regimen. Sleepy, who was six months old when we brought him home, had been weaned normally and fed three meals a day by the breeder—but he also went directly to one meal a day without mishap. Snap, the last of our gang, went to one meal a day at age five months.

Then again, the last three dogs were very small Maltese spaniels, and smaller breeds do mature at a younger age than larger dogs. Even so, there were variations in appetite: Plum and Sleepy always wolfed their food unless they were ill; Inches had a delicate stomach and didn't always finish his meals; Snap always ate, but she took her time. Despite their different feeding habits, there was no perceptible difference in these four dogs' growth, health, or longevity. In fact, the dogs that were fed less frequently at a younger age lived longer.

THE IMPORTANCE OF REGULAR FEEDING

The main reason why self-feeding is unnecessary (and self-defeating) is that dogs so very easily slip into fixed behavior patterns—especially with regard to food. When your veterinarian asks about your dog's eating *habits*, he means just that. A Labrador may bolt his food and a Pekinese eat more slowly, but they'll usually do so consistently from one day to the next. And it's for this reason that watching your dog eat is such an important clue to his well-being; if he's "off his feed," you have to be there to see it.

It's true that wild dogs don't eat on regular schedules, but then, they haven't much choice in the matter. Moreover, wild dogs chew on anything they like, urinate and defecate wherever they please, and generally run wild, restrained only by the limitations of their environment and the social hierarchy of the pack they belong to. In your home, your pet will be only too happy to eat on a regular basis *and* to follow whatever rules that you, his pack leader, demand of him. As long as your dog is going to fall into behavior patterns automatically, they might as well be ones of your choosing.

But won't your dog get hunger pangs if you feed him only once a day? No, because "hunger pangs" are largely a figure of speech. The stomach undergoes regular contractions throughout the day. When empty, the stomach contracts more powerfully, and these movements can be uncomfortably noticeable. But, as you well know, people who habitually skip breakfast seldom suffer hunger pangs, even though their stomachs have had no food since seven or eight o'clock the night before. Why? Because these people are *accustomed* to their particular regimens. You, too, could get by quite well on one meal a day, assuming it was amply nutritious and you were able to digest it properly.

Your hunger—and your dog's—is triggered partly by blood sugar levels but mainly by learned responses and associations. Obviously, a dog can't tell time, but his bodily functions will quickly adapt to given highlights in the twenty-four-hour cycle. And food is such an obsession in a dog's life that he will quickly learn any signal that suggests that chow is on the way. Feed your dog at a given hour, and he'll usually be ready and waiting the next day at the same time. Even in the absence of any dinner bells or other external stimuli, your dog can learn to associate a certain time of day with food. That—and not the sight or smell of his daily meal—is what serves as the trigger.

But once he can anticipate his dinner hour, his digestive system awakens from its relative dormancy and gears itself up. Gastric juices begin flowing, and the stomach and small intestines begin their contractions. *Then* is when hunger pangs may strike. But these warm-up calisthenics of the involuntary muscles ensure better, more complete digestion, which in turn assures regular elimination and vastly easier housebreaking lessons.

On the other hand, constant variations in your dog's feeding times mean that his system never gets the chance to regulate itself. Interestingly, many of the same symptoms a dog displays when fed the wrong foods also show up when he's fed the right diet on an erratic, irregular basis. Deviations often result in obvious and immediate training lapses. But over time, if his body can't set up regular patterns, his various enzymes and hormones can become imbalanced, leading to chronic digestive problems. And it's amazing how little it takes to throw an animal's system out of sync! Every year, dairy farmers petition Congress to repeal daylight saving time on the grounds that the one-hour change confuses their cows and upsets their flow of milk. Dogs, similarly, pay scant attention to official clock time and will stubbornly adhere to their inner biological timetables.

We once received a call from a screenwriter who had

just moved to New York. Back in California, his six-year-old Doberman, Regina, had been the envy of the neighborhood. Though large for a female—tipping the scales at eighty-five pounds—Regina was beautifully proportioned with a wide chest and wasp waist. Prior to the move, the writer had fed Regina regularly each day at ten in the morning and walked her in mid-afternoon, after he'd finished his writing for the day. In New York, though, he decided to alter his schedule and feed her at seven, as soon as he got up to go jogging.

Only a couple of days after getting settled into her new apartment, Regina started to beg for extra helpings; around one o'clock she would start staring at her owner, drooling, and racing back and forth to the kitchen. Since she'd never behaved this way before, the writer decided she must need extra nourishment. Could it be that the New York air had somehow stimulated her appetite? And so he gave in and fed her an extra can of dog food. Within a week or two after she began getting these extra rations, Regina began putting on weight and her behavior changed radically. Instead of being her usual placid, aloof self, she turned into a whining and unhappy dog, nervously licking and chewing herself, and pacing restlessly. Regina was more important to her owner than his new job and he was desperate enough to consider moving back to California. According to the Doberman's internal timetable, she was used to being fed at 10 A.M. Pacific time—1 P.M. Eastern time. When whe was begging for extras at one o'clock, regardless of the full meal she'd been given, she was actually geared up for her normal ten-o'clock feeding—six hours before. Thus, her owner had been conned into feeding her at *both* her "normal" times. No wonder she was putting on weight and displaying the classic behavior changes that come with overfeeding. Worse yet, she wasn't getting walked twice as often, which her increased intake clearly demanded.

Our advice was to feed Regina once a day at her "old" time of 1 P.M., to satisfy her long-running internal clock, and skip the 7 A.M. feeding entirely. Regina's owner had to ignore her early morning begging, which was quite forceful now that she had gotten accustomed to extra food. In addition, he had to feed her less than normal so that she could take off the extra poundage. Within two weeks, Regina had adjusted herself to the new regimen and stopped her nervous behavior—but it took her another two months to trim back down to her old weight.

Before such long-distance moves, it may help to adjust your dog's mealtime forward or backward by about fifteen minutes a day to help eliminate the digestive equivalent of jet lag. Otherwise, a sporadic feeding schedule has dismal side effects on your dog's training, simply because he receives a subliminal but very clear message from the way you feed him. Just having him wait for you to feed him helps establish who's boss—an important point we'll return to in Chapter 7. As most owners quickly discover, a dog is much more apt to pay attention to and obey whoever feeds him his meals. And if he's fed reliably, punctually at the same hour each day, part of this disciplined existence spills over into the rest of his life. You'll find him automatically more amenable to other necessary routines, such as obedience training, housebreaking, and even behaving himself in the presence of others.

CHANGING YOUR DOG'S DIET

One woman fed her 100-pound Scottish deerhound religiously at the same time each day, but she always offered him a slightly different menu. "He needs variety," she told us, "not only for his own pleasure, but to be sure he gets enough nourishment." Her idea of variety meant a different brand and type of dog food *every* day. Her pantry shelves looked like a veritable dog food market, stocked with every exotic food made for dogs. The swing from rich all-meat food to bland all-cereal plus every combination in between was too much for her pet. Unfortunately, this ceaseless change of fare played havoc with the deerhound's innards, and he veered between constipation and diarrhea. On our advice, his owner finally settled on a simple, plain dog food and then stuck to it. Within a week, the dog's digestive problems and eccentricities had vanished, and a month later, he was plainly even better nourished than before.

Variety is tolerable only if it's a habit; you must give your dog the *same* variety of foods all mixed together every day. This way, you guarantee that his digestive tract isn't subject to any sudden surprises and that he's able to benefit from a wide spectrum of different foodstuffs. But the staple of his diet—in most cases, canned dog food—should remain the same.

You needn't worry that your pet will become bored with the same food. Because his sense of smell is so very keen, he can detect the separate odors of all the various ingredients in whatever you serve him. That's more than enough to keep him interested, just as a music lover can listen to the same Beethoven sonata for years, discovering fresh nuances with every hearing.

But what if you *have* to switch your dog's diet, say, at your veterinarian's advice? There are three basic ways to accomplish this kind of change.

Immediate

This is the easiest. Simply switch abruptly to the new fare. If your dog is being fed at his normal time, he's not too likely to worry about the substitution. (And to make sure he's *really* hungry, you might just feed him a few minutes late.) No matter how warm the weather, serve your pet's food at room temperature. Not that he can't digest cold food perfectly well, but the warmer the dog food, the stronger its aroma—and therefore, the more appetizing it will be. To make sure he can smell it, mash it up thoroughly to expose as much of the interior surface as possible (a good practice since it also makes the food easier to digest).

To be on the safe side, give him only about three quarters of his normal ration. This way, he's more likely to finish it all and be hungry for tomorrow's meal—plus, his digestive tract won't have as much new food to cope with its first time out. During any dietary changeover, never give your dog any table scraps or other treats. You want him to focus his interest wholly on the new food, not on any tempting distractions, though you can of course keep on with any vitamin supplements you were feeding him before.

Most active, hungry dogs will eat practically whatever you give them. Besides, if you're switching from dry or semimoist dog food, most dogs will enthusiastically prefer canned. But if you're trying to introduce your pet to a low-fat or other therapeutic diet formulated for health and not for flavor, then things may not go so easily.

If he isn't finishing (or even starting) his new fare, take the new, untouched food away after thirty minutes are up. Above all, don't offer him any compensatory treats to "keep his strength up," because that's exactly what he wants. Remember that your dog can go without food for long periods of time and that this hunger strike was *his* idea, not yours. But keep plenty of fresh water in his dish (going hungry puts an added strain on the kidneys as the body's fat reserves are broken down).

Transitional

If your dog continues to refuse new food for longer than two days, probably the change was too abrupt. After three days, a smaller dog may begin to suffer from malnutrition, so it's important to get him eating again—but on your terms! Simply mix up two parts of the old food he knows and loves and mash in one part of the new. If the resulting mix smells basically like what he's used to, he won't turn it down—especially after a two-day fast. (If your dog's digestion is at all weak, or if he tends to suffer from diarrhea after sudden diet changes, this Transitional method is also the better way to go.) Then, every *other* day, replace about 10 percent of his old food with 10 percent of the new. The idea, of course, is to make the switch slowly and inconspicuously.

Modified

Spoiled, pampered dogs and dogs who've been chronically overfed to the point of obesity, can sometimes prolong a hunger strike until they damage their health. If your pet goes three full days without eating, as a last resort, you can mix a *small* portion of finely chopped turkey or chicken breast with a *small* portion of the new food you want him to eat. Mix them up thoroughly, so he can't pick and choose. Once he wolfs down that mixture—and he will—keep him on the exact same regimen for two or three days. After he eats from his bowl, begin switching the percentages by about 10 percent every day. Just as insurance, sprinkle the new food with liberal doses of an "odor enhancer"—perhaps a bit of poultry fat or chopped kidney or liver.

Once you get your finicky dog eating again, be firm. If you backslide, your pet is sure to also. For at least a month, be sure that any extras or treats are either given as part of his regular meal or "delivered" to the bowl before he's allowed to touch them. If, for medical rasons, you need to change his diet once again, do so very gradually, adding perhaps 5 percent of the new food at each meal and decreasing the old fare proportionately. The point is you don't want your dog to feel he's being punished for having given in the first time, but it's important that he understands that *you* are the one who decides his menu, not he.

In addition, try to boost your dog's appetite by a gentle increase in his normal exercise. If he's on a hunger strike, a couple of extra walks outside may help. Actually, his self-imposed fasting can pay unexpected dividends. Not only may he drop some excess weight, but his stomach may well adjust to lighter bulk, so that he'll be satisfied on slightly less food—an important aid in keeping him at his best possible weight, as we'll explain in the next chapter.

5

Obesity and the Healthfully "Undernourished" Dog

 A celebrated diet doctor, the author of a best-selling book on the subject, once called us to complain that his dogs were nervous chewers—of the rugs, of the sofas, of themselves. We saw that his two German shepherds were clearly overweight and suggested that lighter meals would probably make them feel more comfortable—and let them trim down to a sleeker, more attractive shape. But the doctor belittled our suggestion: "That's their long hair you're looking at. If they were fat, don't you think I'd know it? I wrote the book! You just make them stop chewing."

Technically, any animal who is more than 20 percent above his ideal weight (as recommended for his height and build according to his size and bone structure) is considered obese according to *The Bantam Medical Dictionary*. A veterinarian, Jack Tuttle, of the University of Illinois states that for dogs who are *merely* 20 percent overweight, the mortality rate is 50 percent higher than for their properly slim counterparts. And being only 10 percent overweight still increases a dog's mortality rate by 33 percent. These figures are even more significant when you consider that dogs don't weigh very much to start with: a gain of only three pounds can put a thirty-pound dog in the danger zone.

Why, then, do so many owners overfeed their dogs? One reason, certainly, is that many people associate food with love and affection and hate to "deprive" their pets. Indeed, many clients think it's "cruel" not to feed a dog who's still acting hungry. Of course it's hard to suppress a pang of guilt when your dog looks up from his dish as if to ask, "Is this all?" The problem is that if your dog can't burn up the extra food energy, his body will simply "bank" it in the form of ever-increasing fat reserves. These deposits can quickly become a burden on the lungs and circulatory system, resulting in a tired, unhealthy animal. Too, it may seem intolerably selfish to cook a gourmet meal for your family and give your dog none. (The nursery rhyme about Old Mother Hubbard is pretty well fixed in all our memories.) Besides, dogs are extraordinarily appreciative and seem to get enormous pleasure out of the least scrap we hand them.

But there are motives other than kindness making owners overfeed their dogs. In our society, human obesity is frowned upon; the overweight individual is often considered sloppy, self-indulgent, and lacking in willpower and self-control. This is why many chronically fat people tend to band together and why fatness often runs in families—you feel less self-conscious surrounded by others like yourself. Again and again, we've seen that owners tend to identify with their dogs; obviously, the overweight owner is going to "share" with his pet the food that he himself finds so irresistible.

But even health-conscious individuals, like the diet doctor we met, can overfeed their dogs out of simple ignorance—they have no idea what a fat dog looks like! We all have a pretty good idea of what the ideal human shape should be, since we're constantly exposed to photographs of healthy athletes, actresses in swimsuits, and super-svelte fashion models. But can you recall the last time you saw a picture of an ideal dog— let alone one of the particular breed you own? If you have no mental picture of a properly trim dog, chances are you have no way to judge your own pet.

One owner of a pathetically paunchy Doberman asked us why her animal was so sluggish and hung back when she tried to walk him on a leash. Our reply was that the dog was overweight. "He's not fat," the woman protested, "he's just *big*." To settle the point, we had the Doberman stand up on his hind legs with his forepaws resting on Paul's arm, to reveal a belly that would have been appropriate on Santa Claus. Reluctantly, the owner admitted we were right and resolved to put her dog on a diet.

Clients who see their dogs' sizes as power symbols are particularly hard to work with, and often they have touchy egos that must be handled with care. We won't soon forget the long-distance call we received from an army captain stationed in Florida. His pet bulldog had chewed up the upholstery in his car and wrecked the garage when he was confined for the night, after chewing up most of the furniture in the living room. In desperation the captain finally quartered the dog outside in the yard, where he tried to dig his way under the fence. "He's a big dog," the officer told us, "the biggest bulldog I ever had." That made us wonder: Could the dog actually be fat? We asked for a photograph.

Several days later, a snapshot arrived in the mail. Sure enough, the animal was grossly overweight. When we called back, the captain told us that his dog weighed just over eighty pounds—unheard of for a bulldog!—and was eating seven cups of dry food a day. On our advice, the captain cut his pet's daily ration to two and one-half cans of canned dog food. Within a week, the bulldog's hyperactive behavior was starting to subside and, not too long after, his weight dropped down to around sixty-two pounds, which is far healthier, and just about right for a big, heavy-boned bulldog.

Far too many owners want their dogs to "grow up big and strong" and think that extra helpings are the answer, especially when the animal is still a puppy. It's true that young, growing dogs need extra rations, but they don't need to be chronically *stuffed*.

A client once telephoned to tell us that a canine nutritionist was disputing our advice, insisting that a puppy needs almost nonstop meals of dry food. Intrigued, we made an appointment to talk with the "nutritionist," who turned out to be the 300-pound owner of a pet store that sold pedigreed puppies from a local breeding mill, along with sacks of dry dog food. The man's theory was that unless a puppy is given enough food, he can't possibly grow to his full size and potential.

This is the canine equivalent of the myth that "you have to eat everything on your plate or you won't grow up big and strong." Up to a point, of course, this is true; malnutrition *can* stunt a dog's growth, and the more food he consumes, the more nutrients he's likely to get. But sheer bulk *alone* is no guarantee that he's getting enough nourishment. By way of analogy, atoms of gold are present almost everywhere, even in seawater. But only in gold mines, where rich veins of ore can be found, is the gold concentrated enough to make recovery efforts worthwhile. So it is wih micronutrients; it makes no sense to give your dog three cups of "fortified" dry food to get the same amount of iron present in a small helping of liver.

A nutritious, well-balanced diet will allow a puppy to attain his full size, simply because the ultimate proportions of a dog's muscles and skeletal system are dictated by his genetic makeup. If you want to know how big your puppy is likely to grow, don't look at his paws, look at his parents. For sheer economic reasons, however, many breeders want to get their puppies weaned and into the pet stores as soon as possible, and they have discovered that feeding the puppies more than they really need can prompt them to grow just a little bit faster. But these dogs won't end up any larger than they would have been otherwise. Moreover, a slow, moderate growth rate is best for a growing dog, so that no one part of his body develops out of proportion to any other. For a puppy, excess body fat can be especially harmful since it puts added stress on half-grown joints and tendons, which can hamper proper growth and even cause malformations. Sadly, many of the puppies we saw for sale in the "nutritionist's" shop were large breeds who often suffer from hip dysplasia, a congenital weakness of the hip joints and pelvic girdle caused by careless inbreeding. Any puppy who may be prone to hip dysplasia needs to keep his weight *down* by eating a diet quite different from the one this man was recommending.

Even though your household pet is no longer living his ancestor's feast-or-famine existence, he's still instinctively programmed to wolf down everything you're willing to give him and then to beg for more. And the more he gets above and beyond what he really needs, the more he'll bank as fat that increases his girth and weight but does nothing for his final size, strength, or stamina. In fact, just as humans who become obese eventually develop a host of unhealthy side effects, of which high blood pressure and heart disease are among the most serious, so do dogs; but because of their higher metabolic rate, it will happen even faster to them. Only recently, veterinarians have discovered that surplus weight can affect not just a dog's heart and circulatory system but his liver, kidneys, pancreas, joints, and even his eyesight and hearing. Obesity also lowers a dog's resistance to viruses and bacteria.

Good health is more than a question of just avoiding obesity. Thinness can be *positively* good for an animal. In a laboratory study, just-weaned rats and mice were deliberately "undernourished," that is, given plenty of vitamins and minerals but not as many macronutrients as a control group. To the scientists' surprise, the rodents on the "spartan" diet lived longer and developed fewer degenerative diseases of old age, including cancer. In a follow-up study, the "middle-aged" adult mice were fed a diet rich in micronutrients but with up to 43 percent fewer fats and carbohydrates. These animals promptly lost weight but acted healthier and survived up to 20 percent longer than the control group. Similarly, studies by life insurance companies on the relationship of obesity and life expectancy in humans suggest that it's probably best to be a bit *underweight* from about age sixteen up. (Remember, *The Bantam Medical Dictionary* considers 20 percent over the recommended weight to be obese. Anything less than that is overweight. But neither is a tremendous excess of weight.) Translating these finds to dogs would indicate that your animal should be perhaps 5 percent under his "ideal" body weight after age one.

In 1982, the National Academy of Sciences declared that "dietary restrictions imposed early in life are the only strategy known to increase the life span in warm-blooded animals." A June 1982 article in the *New York Times* reported that a mammal's life span can be lengthened by "undernutrition"—that is, a diet containing plenty of micronutrients, but about 33 percent fewer calories than needed to maintain normal body weight.

The trick, then, is to determine what your dog's ideal weight should be. Unfortunately, the standard weight tables posted in your veterinarian's office aren't as accurate as they could be, since such weights are calculated from relatively inactive animals kept in kennels. As any weight lifter will tell you, lean muscle tissue is heavier than flab. Besides, there are enormous variations within breeds. Generally, a female should weigh less than a male of the same breed, but the proper weight for an individual dog depends on his height, musculature, and bone structure. Many vets admit that the weights they've been recommending for years are simply averages and that an ideal dog probably shouldn't be that heavy. Certainly your veterinarian can give you some guidelines as to what your pet should weigh, but you must make the final judgment based on close observation.

JUDGING THE OVERWEIGHT DOG

Your pet's body should be trim and lean, with a very thin layer of adipose (fatty cells) tissue beneath the skin, which should be supple and elastic in any dog. Run your hands over your dog's ribs: you should be able to feel them easily without having to press down. If his rib cage seems swaddled in fat, chances are he's overweight. The celebrated "pinch test" doesn't work for dogs, because a dog's skin is not attached securely to the underlying tissue. This is an evolutionary adaptation that allows him to move around inside his skin during a fight, so that if he's bitten, his adversary's teeth usually won't penetrate to vital tissue below. This is why most breeds of dogs have "loose pajamas" even after reaching adulthood and why it's easy for you to accumulate a huge roll of loose skin between thumb and forefinger. But if you put pressure on your dog's rib cage and can gather up more than a half inch of the fatty layer *beneath* the skin, then this is a likely sign of obesity.

As anyone who's ever bathed a Pekinese can tell you, long-haired dogs look bigger and bulkier than their short-haired counterparts. But even a chunky-bodied breed like a bulldog or terrier should be firm and muscular. As a last test, stand directly over your dog and look down at his waistline. There should *be* one—a noticeable tuck right behind the rib cage. And as seen from above, his abdomen should be markedly narrower than his chest.

To educate your eye, it also helps to look at pictures of show dogs in kennel club magazines. If your pet is a mixed breed, then look for the closest purebred equivalent. If your dog *is* overweight, extra exercise can help him trim off some of the extra fat (see Chapter 8). But first, some of the extra weight has to come off through dieting, because a dog who is too heavy will have trouble breathing and can overexert himself too easily. A fat dog is simply one who has banked too much food energy; to make him lose weight, you must encourage him to make withdrawals by being sure he burns up more energy than he consumes every day.

For man and beast alike, food energy is measured in terms of the calorie—the amount of heat it takes to raise 1 kilogram of water 1 degree centigrade. Technically, the caloric value of any food is determined by the amount of heat it gives off when burned. As you might expect, fats contribute two and a quarter times as much energy as either proteins or carbohydrates. Specifically, most carbohydrates and proteins each contain about four calories per gram. Many people believe that protein is nonfattening, when actually it has just as many calories per gram as carbohydrates. Nor is it true that the more protein a dog eats the slimmer he will become, or that protein "burns up" fat. It's just that the body is more likely to break down protein for its amino acids, rather than to metabolize it for food energy. Fats, on the other hand, pack a whopping nine calories per gram—which makes them crucial to the success of your dog's diet.

In humans, at least, eating fatty foods provides a

feeling of satisfaction—people often complain that a fat-free diet leaves them feeling hungry. This is probably because fats take a while to emulsify in the small intestine, as well as providing a longer-lasting supply of energy than many sugars. One myth common among human dieters is that starches are fattening too; but in general, any carbohydrates that the body can metabolize quickly are usually the first to be used up. Fats and refined sugars both take the longest to be digested and are the most likely to remain as "spare change" that gets banked rather than gets spent for energy.

It would seem obvious that all fats should be eliminated from the diet of the overweight dog. Unfortunately, the three most important fatty acids—linoleic, linolenic, and arachidic—are all unbankables that must be present in your dog's diet on a regular basis. All occur commonly in nature but are often neglected by dog food manufacturers. For example, most canine diets don't contain nearly enough vegetable oil, in which linoleic acid (especially important for healthy skin and hair) occurs most abundantly.

In a well-balanced, proper diet nearly 95 percent of the fats a dog consumes are absorbed into his bloodstream. If more than 5 percent of ingested fats are excreted, in fact, this may indicate a lack of bile from the liver, malabsorption in the small intestine, or possibly pancreatic insufficiency (see Chapter 11). During digestion, about 10 percent of the fats are immediately broken down into minute droplets of fatty acids that pass through the intestinal wall, acting as "carriers" for the fat-soluble vitamins A, D, E, F, and K. Thus, your dog's diet must contain *some* fats, if only to act as couriers for these important vitamins.

Before beginning any weight-loss program, check with your veterinarian; and certainly don't put your dog on starvation rations, which can cause all sorts of kidney problems and metabolic upsets. If your dog is very overweight, your vet may prescribe a special canned diet food that has only about 300 calories per pound. Or you may prefer to make your dog his own special diet rations, following a recipe developed by Dr. Don Lewis of the Colorado State University Veterinary School.

• Cook 1 cup of lean ground beef, drain off the fat, and allow it to cool to room temperature. Mix with 2 cups *uncreamed* cottage cheese, 8 cups each of canned carrots and canned green beans, and 6 teaspoons of dicalcium phosphate. Dr. Lewis suggests that this mixture be fed in fairly small portions: ⅓ pound for 5-pound dogs to 3½ pounds a day for 100-pound animals. But he suggests dividing this ration into as many as five small meals a day, a practice we wouldn't recommend. A dog may lose weight faster on such a program, but it will play havoc with whatever housebreaking schedule you've worked out (as will be explained in the next chapter).

It shouldn't be hard to lower your dog's weight by feeding him a diet of commercial canned dog food—as long as you count the calories and limit the amount he eats. The average adult dog needs about thirty calories per day per pound of body weight. So for a forty-pound dog to lose weight, you have to be sure he gets *fewer* than 30 × 40, or 1200, calories per day. Suppose you want this forty-pound dog to drop five pounds. You have to then calculate what a thirty-five-pound dog should be eating—that is, 1050 calories—and then deduct another 20 percent for the duration of the diet, which reduces his daily intake to only 840 calories. To streamline these calculations, simply take your dog's *ideal* weight and multiply by 24; the result will be the number of calories he should be getting until he attains that figure.

The label on any dog food can will usually list the total calories. If it doesn't, you can easily determine the calorie content for yourself. For once, disregard all the micronutrients on the label and write down *only* the stated percentages of protein, carbohydrates, and fats. Then multiply the percentages of protein and carbohydrates by 4 and the fats by 9. The total of the three sums will give you the number of calories per 100 grams. There are 454 grams to the pound, so to convert that metric total to the number of calories per pound, multiply the calories 100 grams figure by 4.5.

Here's how it works. One brand of dry food formulated for adult dogs contains 25 percent crude protein, 15 percent fats, 3.5 percent crude fiber, 10 percent moisture, and 10 percent ash. In this roster, you use only the protein and fats for calculation. Twenty-five percent protein times 4 is 100 and 15 percent fats times 9 is 135 for a total of 235 calories per 100 grams. To determine the number of calories per pound, multiply 235 by 4.5 for a total of 1147.5 calories.

As another example, take a canned food intended for older dogs with lower calorie requirements. Here, the label reads, "Protein 20%, Fat 10%, Fiber 5% and

Water 50%"—for a total of 170 calories per 100 grams, or only 765 calories per pound.

Notice, however, that no carbohydrates were listed on the label of either food. It may be that carbohydrates are regarded as a normal part of other ingredients and don't merit a separate listing. But it's more likely that they don't need to be mentioned at all—the National Research Council has stated that if a diet contains enough glucose precursors (that is, substances the liver can easily convert to glucose), there's no evidence that carbohydrates are necessary. In fact, the council gives no minimum requirement for carbohydrates, only a maximum limit—which means there's no minimum requirement at all.

Note that both the canned and dry foods have a percentage of contents unaccounted for on the labels: the dry dog food is missing 36.5 percent and the canned food 15 percent. It makes sense to assume that these secret ingredients are in fact carbohydrates, so figure them into the total at a rate of 4 calories per gram. When these unknowns are counted in, you can estimate that the canned food contains 1035 calories per pound and the dry food has around 1804. (Water has no calories, of course, and after presoaking, the dry dog food will expand, lowering both its calorie-per-pound rate and its nutrient value.)

In figuring out the daily ration for a dieting canine, be sure to count the caloric value of his morning breakfast biscuits. You should definitely cut out any between-meal snacks, tastes, or treats you've been giving your dog—which may be the whole reason for his obesity in the first place. If you feel conscience-stricken, give him a vitamin supplement to assure that he's not being shortchanged on any important micronutrients. But don't give him vitamins with sugar coatings or starchy binders, and remember that some vitamins *themselves* can contain substantial amounts of calories. One tablespoon of lecithin granules, for example, contains 50 calories, and a single lecithin capsule contains 8. Wheat germ contains thiamine (also known as vitamin B_1, which helps metabolize glucose) as well as 3.63 calories per gram. Yeast, with its high B-vitamin content, has a hefty 300 calories per tablespoon.

Despite your dog's inbred preoccupation with food, dieting is probably much easier for him than it is for you. Unless he simply isn't eating (as after an illness or when on a hunger strike for forbidden food), you shouldn't be able to detect any change in his energy level. If anything, a slightly hungry dog should be *more* active than one who's been overfed. If he's been devoting a good part of his day to digestion, the new edge of mild hunger will make him more restless and inquisitive. As he starts to trim down, his energy will continue to increase.

But how will you know how well his diet's progressing? Most people know their own weight, but when asked how much their dog weighs, their estimate often runs ten pounds in either direction, which is quite a difference, when the average dog weighs a mere thirty pounds! Unless you *know* your dog's present poundage as well as what he should weigh, it's going to be difficult to feed him properly.

Your veterinarian should be able to judge, from your dog's build, how much of his total weight is fat that he can afford to lose. And once-a-week weighings can give you plenty of feedback that lets you make adjustments in your dog's rations. But even obedient dogs don't like to sit on a scale. To weigh a fairly small dog, pick him up, stand on the scale, and read your combined weight; then weigh yourself and subtract that. For a larger dog, you can stretch the area of a bathroom scale by using a sheet of plywood, or else take him to the veterinarian (or to a local shipping company or courier service with industrial scales).

You probably won't *see* any immediate change in your dieting pet's appearance. Like humans, dieting dogs may not begin losing weight right away, since it may take up to a week for fat deposits to halt and start running in the other direction. But given a dog's relatively small body size, the loss of only a pound or two is the equivalent of a ten- or twenty-pound loss in a human being. After two or three weeks, you should be able to notice a definite slimming down. (Polaroid or Instamatic snapshots will help refresh your memory.)

Even after your dog reaches his ideal weight, it will pay you to disregard "helpful" advice from friends and relatives who may have their own preconceptions of how an animal should look. "Isn't he eating?" "He must be starving to death!" "Look at how thin he's getting." These remarks can weaken your resolve to have a slim and healthy pet. The answer, of course, is simply to take your dog to the scales and weigh him again—numbers don't lie!

While you're trying to lower your dog's weight, remember that he can't possibly understand what the diet is trying to accomplish. He may feel more alert and active but certainly won't connect that with his newly reduced rations. All he'll know for sure is that he's not getting the same volume he's used to, and he'll be even more tempted to seek out extras on his own. You must be alert to see that he eats no more than what you give him. Don't let him beg from friends and neighbors who may be willing to help him cheat on his diet—and make sure no one else is undermining your efforts.

One time we got a call from a sleek fashion model who complained that Tiffany, her once svelte saluki, was gaining weight even though her daily meal had been cut nearly in half. The woman had already taken Tiffany to the vet, who confessed he wasn't an expert in thyroid conditions and recommended she consult a number of specialists. The ever-increasing Tiffany had been given tests galore to no avail. Then the dog was being given only a few tablespoons of food a day, but still she lost no weight.

When we arrived at the woman's town house, the definitely chubby saluki contrasted sharply with her fashionably thin owner. The woman showed us how much she was feeding Tiffany, and we agreed it was scarcely enough to sustain a Chihuahua. Obviously the saluki was getting rations—elsewhere. But the model lived alone in her brownstone—there was no doorman, dog walker, or boyfriend who could be plying the dog with extras. In fact, Tiffany's owner didn't even keep biscuits or dog candy in the house. The way she kept *her* figure was to make sure the refrigerator contained no temptations. "The only time there's extra food around is when my nephew comes to visit. He lives down the street. When my brother and his wife go out, he comes over here to watch movies on my video recorder."

We discovered that the boy was a sort of culinary

surrogate; whenever he visited, his aunt would cook for him the kind of rich gourmet meals that her own stringent diet wouldn't allow her to consume. Lately she'd been doing a lot of cooking because her brother and his wife had computerized their records at their trucking business and they were out four nights a week taking a crash course in computer technology. After a quick interview with the nephew, we learned that he greatly preferred submarine sandwiches. But to avoid hurting his aunt's feelings, he would slip most of his salmon mousse and veal scallopini under the table to Tiffany. When the model stopped cooking for the boy, the saluki's weight rapidly returned to normal.

This owner had a sound idea, though: when you or your dog are on a diet, make sure there's no extra food lying about to provide temptation. One client who owned two cats had a real problem trying to get her Jack Russell terrier down to his proper fifteen-pound weight. At a hefty twenty-one pounds, the dog was almost 50 percent obese, solely from snacking on the cat food that the woman left out. Cats are not gluttons and can be allowed to self-feed. In this case, however, it was the terrier who was doing the self-feeding; and before his owner caught on, she would heap even more semimoist food in the bowl for her "ravenously hungry" cats. Cat food is even richer in protein than dog food, so the terrier wound up banking more of this extra nourishment. (That's yet another argument against giving your dog any extras—treats and tidbits are nearly always richer and more fattening than your pet's staple fare.)

Our task, then, was to figure out how to keep the terrier out of the cats' bowl. We tried setting it up high on the kitchen counter, but the terrier soon learned to leap the distance after watching the cats do it a few times. In spite of his extra poundage, this dog was amazingly agile, and he also had made good friends with one of the cats. If he wasn't able to reach the cats' bowl, the cat would obligingly shove it onto the floor for him.

This case may sound far-fetched, but then there's hardly any *normal* way that dogs go off their diets. Finally we told the woman that the simplest answer would be to take her cats off their self-feeding regimen and put them on a schedule of fixed mealtimes—with the terrier out of the room while they ate. After a week of this system, the cats were still doing fine, and the terrier had begun to lose weight.

Expect an average-sized dog to attain his proper weight in about two and a half months. Then you can gradually increase his food. But do so slowly, continuing to weigh your pet every week so that you can stabilize or reduce his intake whenever you discover him putting on weight again. Once your dog is properly thin, all you now need to do is discover the exact quantity of food that will *maintain* that trim, slim silhouette. Some breeders let their dogs go without food one day a week, providing them with water only, to ensure that the animals don't gain weight and to let them "clean out their systems." But not having had any experience with this technique, we can't recommend it. To us, it makes much better sense to feed a dog sensibly so that he doesn't need one-day fasts to even things out.

THE MAINTENANCE DIET

If all people fed their pets according to the directions on the dog food labels almost all dogs would be obese, since manufacturers advise that you serve 25 to 50 percent more than your dog really needs.

Compared to you, a dog does need more calories per pound of body weight. That's partly because his metabolism is faster. Normal human body temperature is 98.6° F., but a dog's is 102° F. In a sense, then, your pet is running a healthy fever and will thus burn up calories at a slightly faster rate.

The National Research Council gives a wide range of daily canine requirements, from twenty-three calories per pound for a fifty-pound dog up to sixty-one calories per pound for a two-pound pet. But these tables are general guidelines that deliberately ignore individual differences. As one brochure puts it, such requirements reflect "the diet of the mature dog at rest . . . kept under average conditions in urban homes." But as you know, growing puppies need two to three times as many calories as adults of the same weight, simply because they're using up so much energy in the growth process alone. A week-old puppy needs about sixty calories a day per pound of body weight to assist in creating new muscle, bone, and connective tissue. By three weeks, his needs will have risen to more than eighty calories per pound, and thereafter, he may need more than ninety. But a good percentage of these daily calories should be in the form of protein, to help him grow.

Fortunately, a sixty-pound dog doesn't need to eat six times as much as a ten-pound animal. In fact, an adult dog's energy requirements are inversely proportional to his size. In other words, the heavier your dog, the fewer calories per pound of body weight he needs to consume. For example, a dog weighing only two and a quarter pounds may require about sixty-four calories/pound per day, while a pet weighing twenty-two and a half pounds will need only thirty-four calories/pound. In dog food terms, this means that a ten-pound pooch needs between one-half and two-thirds of a can, while a hundred-pound dog will need three to four cans. And between the two, a sixty-five-pound pet will do fine on two to two and a half cans, plus biscuits in the morning.

DIETARY QUANTITY OF FOOD FOR ADULT DOGS

Body Weight (in pounds)	Cans of Moist Food *or* Packages of Semimoist Food *or* Cups of Dry Food (after Soaking)
5	⅓
15	½ to ⅔
20 to 30	1 to 1¼
35 to 50	1½ to 2
55 to 65	2 to 2½
70 to 100	3 to 4

Although there's no hard-and-fast "right" amount for any individual dog, we do advise you to *base* your dog's daily rations on those shown in this table.

As with most other aspects of canine behavior, it's

up to you to set the standards and see that your dog abides by them. Your long-term goal, again, is to maintain the dog's weight at just below "normal" throughout his life, which will necessitate a few adjustments along the way. A dog's caloric needs will vary according to his size, age, and activity level, as well as the season of the year. Obviously, a well-exercised animal will burn up more calories than before, when he was obese and dieting. A dog who sleeps outdoors in winter or who lives in a cold, wet climate needs more calories to stoke and maintain his 102° body temperature. Similarly, a dog who is fox hunting, herding sheep, or pulling a sled across the snow will want more food than a sedentary pet who sleeps most of the day. But if such a fast-track dog gets more quick-energy carbohydrates, he'll also need greater quantities of micronutrients to keep his system running at peak efficiency. Specifically, the more carbohydrates your dog ingests, the more vitamin B_1 he'll need to help him metabolize them.

On the other hand, an older dog's metabolism is at least 20 percent lower than a younger adult's, so you'll want to taper off his rations after he passes the age of eight (see Chapter 12). Remember, too, that having been spayed is not an excuse for a female dog to put on weight, any more than having been castrated is one for a male dog. Such operations may quiet the dogs' behavior, but that's just a signal for you to decrease their calories accordingly. But neither is cold weather or lots of exercise an automatic signal to allow your dog more food. That's why you should be weighing him each week. If your dog is clearly hungry, increase his rations by perhaps 10 percent—but if you detect even a slight weight increase as a result, chop his meals back to their previous volume.

THE TRULY UNDERWEIGHT AND HYPERTHYROID DOG

A dog's body weight is not influenced solely by food intake. Thus while a slight weight loss is nothing to worry about, any sudden or chronic drop in poundage is a warning that something may be seriously wrong— perhaps worms (see Chapter 9) or a digestive disorder.

Very few dogs are actually underweight unless they've been ill or have been living as strays after having been lost or abandoned by their owners. Check with your vet to see whether a "found" dog or puppy needs extra carbohydrates in the form of pasta or cooked grains. A good quality protein might also be needed for any tissue rebuilding. And a double dose of vitamin supplements will ensure adequate nourishment, while letting the dog put on weight slowly and naturally.

Sudden obesity, on the other hand, can result from a hormone problem, the best known of which is *hypothyroidism*, or below-normal functioning of the thyroid gland, resulting in sluggish metabolism. Of course, far too many people use "a thyroid condition" or "a glandular problem" as an excuse for being overweight— and they use the same excuse for their pets. A veterinarian can do a blood test to determine if your dog's thyroid is working properly. Should the gland be out of sync, the problem is not so much what he's eating as how his body is utilizing that nourishment. Therefore, you should stabilize his diet as much as possible—no treats, no extras, no changes—to let your vet see clearly the effects of whatever medications he prescribes.

In short, the fewer calories you feed your adult dog, the healthier he'll be. In a sense, this regimen is the exact flip side of malnutrition; overall low calorie count, together with plenty of well-balanced micronutrients is the answer.

6
Housebreaking the Diet-Assisted Way

 Some people are so interested in caloric intake as a measure of their dogs' daily ration that they entirely forget to consider the sheer bulk involved. At one of the classes we taught at a local ASPCA, a man brought his ten-month-old schnauzer who weighed about twelve pounds. He'd been feeding this dog four cups of dry dog food a day (the amount recommended on the bag) and couldn't fathom why the schnauzer still wasn't housebroken. The only way he could house-train the animal, we explained, was if he stayed home and took the dog out about a dozen times a day, since that was how many times the dog needed to defecate.

The *volume* of a dog's food has little relation to how many nutrients are absorbed in the small intestine. Therefore, it should be obvious that the less your dog eats and drinks, the less often he'll have to relieve himself. Thus the "undernourishment" regimen we just outlined fits in very neatly with your housebreaking plans. Indeed, *the* key to successful housebreaking is to feed your dog a proper amount of food to start with. That way, he can learn to time his daily eliminations to when you're going to be home to let him out.

With puppies, there's a very short time lag between feeding and elimination. Just-weaned puppies usually urinate just *before* eating. Give a slightly older puppy something to eat or drink, and he's sure to eliminate a few moments later. With very young dogs, it therefore makes sense to follow feeding times with a prompt lesson in indoor paper training. Later in your dog's life, he'll be able to adapt himself to your schedule, more or less. But for a puppy, it'll make things easier if you follow his lead.

To help housebreak a new puppy, keep his paper-training area at a good distance from his bed and where you feed him. Even very young puppies have an instinct for cleanliness and will leave their rest area (or try to) before relieving themselves. But for a dog to develop and maintain this instinct depends largely on his sense of smell. If both the puppy and his living quarters are not kept clean, he may become habituated to the odor of urine and not perceive any difference between his nest and where he relieves himself. Thus it's important to be sure a puppy is always fresh smelling, that he doesn't get urine or feces on his paws, and that his environment is kept clean. (If you have more than one puppy, give each one his own bed. This will facilitate cleanliness and also ensure that each one rests well.)

Smell discrimination is one reason why dogs raised or boarded in a kennel often have housebreaking lapses later on. If they are conditioned to live close to their own waste, they won't develop the same sensitivity that a single dog, in the company of humans, will swiftly adopt.

Your most important responsibility, then, is to *prevent* accidents, simply because in his first few weeks of life, practically everything a young dog does is a learning experience and his every action is a potential habit. When it comes to older dogs, housebreaking is *strictly* a matter of habit. In the wild, adult dogs will regularly defecate a good distance from where they sleep, not only for sanitary reasons but also to mark the limits of their territory. Therefore, a dog's instinct is to spread his waste products as widely as possible; your whole effort at housebreaking is to instill just the opposite message. The easiest way to nip "territorial" elimination in the bud is to provide one single, constant, unequivocal spot where your dog can relieve himself. After several weeks, ingrained habit will tend to overrule the promptings of other instincts, and when you take him outside the sights and smells of his usual place will stimulate him to comply. Once again, it's up to you to set the rules.

A puppy who's fed twice a day will have two bowel movements a day—at least. Ideally, then, you should make sure he defecates every evening just before bedtime, because you don't want him to have to relieve himself before morning. This is a crucial goal to shoot for, because as soon as your dog can hold out through the night, you know that he'll be able to last through the day if you're away.

As a dog becomes an adult, he'll need to relieve himself less and less frequently—assuming, that is, that you're cutting down on the number and quantity of feedings, as we outlined in Chapter 4. We learned of one woman who assumed that her tiny, high-strung Chihuahua puppies needed a constant supply of energy to keep them going and that they were far too small to consume enough nourishment in only one sitting. Accordingly, she fed them a diet that would have made sense for a human with low blood sugar— five or six small meals a day. After two years, the dogs still weren't housebroken, simply because they had to go too often for her to be able to walk them in time.

WATER AND KIDNEY FUNCTION

Water is an essential component of all living things. Your dog's body, by weight, is about 70 percent water, much of it being in the form of blood, which is 88 percent H_2O. Bone is 25 percent water, and even those solid-looking teeth have a 10 percent moisture content. In addition, a dog's digestive tract uses water as its basic solvent for acid and enzymes; and gastric juices are approximately 97 percent water.

We once knew a cat, the pampered pet of a local butcher, who never drank water—his diet of fresh raw liver gave him all the liquid he needed. Kangaroo rats (small rodents with long hind legs that jump like kangaroos, living in arid areas of western North America) and some desert-living deer are able to produce so much water internally, as a by-product of their normal metabolism, that they don't need to drink. Your dog also produces a small amount of water in the process of burning up fats and carbohydrates and protein, but the amount is a drop in the bucket compared with his total needs.

Wild dogs may not eat regularly, but several times a day they will lap water from creeks and ponds. For even if they get plenty of moisture in their food, and while nearly all the water they drink is absorbed into their systems, their bodies are constantly losing water. At least 20 percent of the moisture your dog drinks is breathed out again via his lungs—and even more than that in hot weather, when he pants to cool himself. Whereas short-haired mammals like horses, and people, use sweat evaporation to lower their body temperatures, a dog sweats mainly on the soles of his feet and on his nose (if he sweated in a human fashion, the moisture would simply soak into his fur without providing any cooling). He lowers his body temperature mainly through panting—expelling hot air from the lungs and letting saliva evaporation cool the blood in his lolling tongue. This method is not superbly efficient, but it does cause him to lose quantities of body moisture.

Almost all the rest of the water your dog loses is through his urine which is 93 percent water on average. You can expect your adult female dog to urinate approximately three or four times a day. But because an adult male dog uses his urine for marking territory, he may urinate as many as several dozen times on each of his walks. Your only worry is whether he *can* save it until he gets outside.

The specific quantity of water that a dog requires will vary according to his activity, the ambient temperature and humidity, and the kind of food he's eating; and naturally the season of the year can slow or hasten loss of water from the body. In this case, self-feeding (or should we say self-drinking?) is necessary; your dog needs a constant supply of drinking water at all times. In fact, if you keep his dish brimful, it will prevent him from getting thirsty and gulping down more than he really needs.

For simple convenience, keep his water dish fairly close to a sink in the bathroom, kitchen, or basement—ideally, on a tile or linoleum floor where occasional drops will do no damage. A dog with long floppy ears, such as a Pekinese or a cocker spaniel may need a dish with higher sides to keep his ears dry, but remember that a short-muzzled dog may have trouble getting to the bottom of a narrow container. Most owners find it convenient to keep the dog's water dish beside his food bowl. (The only drawback to keeping it in the bathroom is that taller dogs will take to lapping from the toilet unless you remember to keep the seat down.)

Because water is transparent, you can't always easily see when a water dish is empty, so be sure to check the water level at least once a day and more often in hot weather. Snap, our Maltese, used to push her water dish around the floor to tell us that it was empty. Other dogs will simply lie down next to the empty dish, much as thirsty animals will camp by a dried-up water hole and wait for rain. Even if your dog doesn't finish the water you leave for him, be sure to change the water at least once a day.

Since water doesn't have to be digested, it doesn't need to be prepared in any way for your dog to make use of it. But you should be aware that many municipal water supplies are laced with chlorine and other germicidal substances that are so strong that water fresh from the tap will kill tropical fish. These chemicals quickly boil away during cooking, but at room temperature or refrigerated they may take up to a day or two to evaporate or decompose. If the quality of your local water is questionable, you may want to boil your dog's drinking water and let it cool off before giving it to him, or let it stand in a pitcher or open jar in the refrigerator for a day or so. As a last resort, allow your dog to drink the same bottled water that you enjoy. Make sure you use spring water. (Distilled water is not good. It lacks many of the important trace elements found in spring water. Not only does distilled water taste flat by comparison, but it may also contribute to circulatory problems.)

IS WATER ENOUGH?

"How would you like to drink nothing but water all your life?" is the advertising slogan of a "beef-flavored" drink, alleged to be full of nutrients, that was introduced in 1982 for owners to serve their dogs in place of water. We'd advise against it, though. First of all, it contains a great deal of fructose; and, as the advertising says, "If he likes it, he'll drink more"—probably more than he really needs. It's better for your dog to get his nutrients from solid food. On the other hand, it *is* important to serve him the liquid in which his food has been prepared. Water-soluble nutrients (especially sugars, vitamins B and C, and certain minerals) dissolve quickly during cooking.

There are a few times when you should withhold water from your dog. An animal who is retching or vomiting shouldn't be allowed to drink, lest he accidentally inhale water. Emptying his water dish just before a car ride can forestall motion sickness. And it's all right to deprive him of water just before your bedtime when he's being house-trained.

Lastly, it's a good idea to rinse out his water dish during mealtime and not replace it until a bit later. Your dog's food should contain plenty of water to begin with. If he drinks on top of eating, this will further dilute the hydrochloric acid in his gastric juices, which can interfere with his digestion. In turn, improperly digested carbohydrates can ferment, causing bloat or excessive gas. So about half an hour after his meal, when his stomach has done most of its mechanical churning work, you can let him drink again.

Aside from these instances, always provide your dog with as much water as he wants. On the other hand, it's perfectly all right to regulate his *desire* for water! For example, salty and protein-rich foods will induce your pet to drink more to help his kidneys handle the extra salts and nitrogenous wastes. One winter, a young woman trying to housebreak a young basset hound discovered her puppy was suddenly drinking much more and urinating to excess. There had been a heavy snowfall two days before, and the streets had been strewn with rock salt. The puppy had tracked some of the salt inside on his paws, licked it off, and developed a raging thirst. Some rawhide chew-toys also contain salt (though it's not marked on the label) and can serve as the motivation for a suddenly thirsty pet.

For reasons we've already explained, dry food also encourages a dog to drink more than he needs. One client who owned a twelve-pound Jack Russell terrier complained that the dog was drinking enough for a Great Dane. Every time she checked, the water dish was bone dry, and she'd have to fill it again. Finally, fearing that the dog might have kidney problems, she took him to the veterinarian, who could find nothing wrong. We asked her what kind of food the terrier was eating—and, sure enough, it was a dry mix. Within a few days after switching to canned food the dog began drinking less water, and within a week his intake was down to what was normal for an animal his size.

Feeding either canned food or presoaked dry food will cut down on your dog's need to drink extra. But be sure that the canned food is moist enough for your pet to eat. Meat from a butcher or a slaughterhouse has been drained of blood and other body fluids and is much drier than what a dog would consume in the wild. Again, most brands of canned dog food contain about 75 percent water, but this really isn't enough. When these foods first came on the market, the directions on most labels called for adding at least another quarter of a can of water to make "gravy." We consider the ideal consistency to be that of a thick chili or stew.

A number of health problems are signaled by a dog's suddenly drinking and urinating more than usual. If his kidneys have been weakened by infection, toxic chemicals, or just age, they can lose their ability to concentrate wastes from the blood and will require more water to let them do their work. Extra drinking can also be a sign of the onset of diabetes (the kidneys require more water to flush unmetabolized sugar from the bloodstream) or Cushing's disease (a hormonal disorder in which the adrenal glands secrete too much steroid hormones; afflicted dogs usually develop pot-bellies, act lethargic, and display dry skin and thinning fur).

Another dog who needs prompt veterinary attention

is one who strains but releases very little urine. Because of their short urethras, female dogs often suffer bladder infections, which are best treated with antibiotics, plus vitamin C to acidify the urine and kill the bacteria. Urine that is bloody indicates kidney injury or bladder stones, which require immediate surgery, as well as a subsequent change in diet to prevent recurrences.

THE BASICS OF HOUSEBREAKING

Compared to human childhood, a dog's puppyhood is very brief: three human years are the equivalent of three canine months. By age three, your child should be toilet-trained; by three months, then, so should your dog be housebroken.

Until he's entirely trustworthy, don't give him the run of the house. Keep him on a short chain leash. Simply clip one end of the leash to your dog's regular buckle collar—*not* a choke chain, on which he might actually choke himself. Take the other end of the leash and attach that to an eye hook you've screwed tightly into the floor or baseboard in each of the spots you've selected to confine your pet during training. Or attach the leash to a permanent object by looping it around and tying the leash. Pick areas to confine your dog where he will be out of the way but not out of contact with the rest of your household. Use your common sense, don't put him near a heater, fan, radiator, or electric wiring. It is a good idea to keep him beside your bed at night on a rubber mat to prevent damage from any mistakes he might make. Give him a bed, water, and chew bones where he is confined to make sure he is comfortable. At first give your dog only limited freedom from the leash and only when you can watch him. As training progresses and he is behaving himself and doing as you want, give him more. This isn't punishment, just prevention—if he learned as a puppy not to foul his nest, that instinct will now work to your advantage.

Your most practical option is to teach a dog to relieve himself outside. But if your puppy hasn't yet had all his inoculations, put a pile of newspaper right outside your front door. Carry the dog to the paper and set him down on it. Use the leash to keep him on the paper. If he drifts off the paper, gently pull him back on it with the leash, but don't jerk on the leash or pull angrily. If he does nothing, take him back in and confine him, then take him out again an hour later. Eventually he will go outside when given the chance.

If the dog is stubborn about defecating where and when he's supposed to—or just to hasten things along—moisten the plain ends of cardboard matches in saliva and insert them into your dog's rectum, head side out so that they are half in and half out. (A Maltese might need only two or three matches, while a German shepherd will require a half dozen.) If he can't turn around to get at them with his teeth, he'll promptly defecate to get rid of them. Some people speculate that stimulation to make a dog defecate may lead to chronic constipation. They feel that the dog's system will get so used to external aid to get going that without such aid it won't work. Not so, although suppositories that are inserted high up into the rectum might cause dependence. Our method, however, doesn't do that; it mimics the natural system used by a mother dog to make him eliminate when and where she wants—she licks around the anus of a young pup. The matches are inserted only halfway and are designed to act as a stimulus around the tip of the anus. Both actions create the urge in the dog to relieve himself so that if he needs to he will; they do not force the issue as does a suppository. Moreover, our method allows you to set up a conditioned response so that you can teach your dog to actually go in one particular spot or at one particular time. Simply use the matches where or when you want him to go and he will associate the area or time with elimination—even when the stimulus isn't used.

Although your dog may have had all his inoculations, putting paper down outside gives him a specific trigger, especially if you place previously soiled paper atop the new. This method is particularly useful if you have to clean up after your dog: simply roll up the paper and deposit the entire bundle in the nearest trash can. (As we'll explain in Chapter 9 it's important to dispose of your dog's feces even if your community doesn't have a cleanup law; this will help keep your dog and other animals from contracting roundworms and other intestinal parasites.) Thereafter, you can walk him as a treat, but only *after* he's done what he's supposed to.

Whenever your dog does as expected, *where* you expected, overwhelm him with praise. Let him run about some, then take him back inside; play with him and give him a taste of freedom to show him what he can anticipate when he's fully housebroken. But when you can no longer be with him, confine him again. Conversely, correct him sternly when he misbehaves. It's always best if he receives an immediate reprimand for mistakes; but even if you don't catch him in the act, always punish him—and make sure he understands why. Set up paper towels and white vinegar beside his mess.* Holding his collar, lead him over to the scene of the crime. (Never call a dog to punish him or he's likely not to obey you in the future.) Holding him firmly between your legs, make him watch as you clean the floor. Then sprinkle some vinegar on the site; the sharp smell will remind him of urine, but this will be a smell he associates with you. Next touch a drop of vinegar to your dog's nose. Then give him one hard slap, hold his nose to the spot on the floor, and let him go—all to be forgiven. If he wanders back that way, the lingering vinegar smell will remind him of your displeasure.

Once your dog no longer misbehaves inside, you can consider him trained. But don't be too quick to give him the run of the house. Let him earn his freedom, as he discovers that each room is your territory and not a potential free zone for him. Most often a healthy dog who suddenly urinates indoors does so aggressively, to claim his turf and pull rank (as when a strange dog or person visits his home). You must counter with swift punishment to reassert your dominance, or else the dog will swiftly unlearn all the housebreaking lessons you've taught him.

If you have more than one dog in the household and don't know which one misbehaved, punish them both, or else the innocent dog may quickly pick up the habit

---

*Readers of our earlier books will recall that we advocated Tabasco sauce on the dog's gums as punishment. This really isn't necessary; your slap and displeasure are deterrents enough.

from his errant playmate. But if one dog is defecating and you want to be sure of the culprit, feed one of the dogs shredded raw carrots with his food to color-code his feces with orange flecks.

Now your only concern should be that your perfectly trained dog doesn't become motivated to start chewing on the furniture or himself. This isn't likely to happen as long as he's getting the right type and quantity of food, as we've already outlined. But if you find your dog is licking his paws or other body parts or worrying them with his front teeth *and* halts this behavior as soon as he's taken outside to relieve himself, then he simply needs more opportunities so that he doesn't have to control himself that long.

THE RIGHT SCHEDULE

One of our clients decided to feed her two-year-old Labrador early in the morning before she left for work. She had read that it was healthier for people to eat a hearty breakfast, so why shouldn't the same be true for dogs? Besides, this new schedule would give him all the rest of the day to digest it, so she could take him for a vigorous run when she came home in the evening. But to her dismay, the dog's behavior rapidly deteriorated and he began chewing on the upholstery of her apartment furniture.

It's important to note that this dog was getting canned dog food, in amounts that were exactly right for his size. We explained to his owner that, because the ingestion of new food stimulates the entire digestive tract, a dog usually needs to be walked within a matter of hours after his daily meal. This was one well-trained

Labrador; we had personally supervised his house-breaking. Knowing better than to relieve himself indoors, the dog took up chewing to distract himself from his urges and internal discomfort. When his owner switched him back to an evening meal that let her walk him about five hours after he ate, he quickly stopped chewing without any further reprimands.

If your dog is eating only one meal a day, then all of it should finish the digestion process at about the same time. As a general rule, he'll defecate about five hours after eating, and again twelve hours or so later. Therefore, it's important that you figure in these elapsed times when planning your feeding and walking schedules. If you feed your dog at 6 P.M., for example, be ready to walk him around eleven that night and again around seven the next morning.

To a degree, then, the best time to feed your dog depends on your schedule, and when you *know* you'll have enough time to walk him. If you have a 9-to-5 job, plan to take your dog out in the morning right after you get up, before his morning biscuits, and again as soon as you return home, *before* you feed him. (A full bladder is more compelling than an empty stomach.) If you work at home or can get back by late afternoon, then serve his daily meal around four. In any case, try to maintain the same eight-hour time lapse between biscuits and dinner.

Most people find it most convenient to take the dog out first thing in the morning, again in the afternoon or early evening (usually when the owner gets home from work), and a third and last time before turning in. This isn't to say you can't walk your dog at other times, but any extra walks should be just that and not substitutes for his regular outings. And because your dog is a creature of habit, it's vital that you walk him at the exact same times each day. Dogs are instinctively receptive to the differences between night and day; because of temperature changes, the day smells different to him. But more important, he's a pack animal and will readily adjust his schedule to yours, just as his domestic ancestors have been doing for thousands of years. He'll want to stay home at night and sleep—and that's when his digestive tract should be allowed a rest too.

Scheduling the walk times as precisely as possible makes it vastly easier for him to control himself. If he *knows* he'll get to go out every evening at 6:00, rain or shine, he'll be better able to hold out those last few minutes and less likely to start chewing out of nervousness. Remember that if *you* forget, it's not your animal's fault. Several years ago, a friend of ours was having such a good time at her own New Year's Eve party that she entirely forgot about her nightly eleven-o'clock commitment to her St. Bernard and was punished by the sight of her dog defecating in the hall—right on the stroke of midnight.

We always took our four dogs out at 7 A.M., again at 5 or 6 P.M., and one final time at 11 P.M. Every so often, their morning walk would be delayed by half an hour or so, and if we knew we'd be out late in the evening, we always made sure to walk them one last time before leaving home, so that if their final walk of the day got delayed, it wouldn't cause any problems. It's okay to depart from the fixed schedule every so often as long as you add "compensation" walks so that your dog enjoys the same number of outings—but then get back to your former schedule as soon as possible. If your own schedule is hopelessly erratic, provide your dog with at least two walks, morning and night, that he can depend on.

In a few, infrequent cases, a dog's misbehavior in the house will be not aggression but exactly the reverse. A terrified or extremely submissive dog will often urinate or defecate involuntarily, as part of the age-old fight-or-flight reaction. The only way to avoid such lapses is to remove the source of the anxiety *and* bolster your dog's confidence with praise. Also, be sure you know who is disciplining the dog; if one person allows him to get away with lapses, he'll never be trained properly. In a particularly knotty case, a woman moved in with her new boyfriend and brought along her female Australian sheepdog, who suddenly began piddling all over the house. After long questioning, it turned out that the boyfriend deeply resented the dog's habit of climbing up on his couch (in her owner's apartment, she had been allowed up on the furniture) and punished the animal harshly whenever he found hairs on the pillows. Naturally, he did so when the dog's owner wasn't around. As a result, the dog became terrified of this man and would leave spots whenever she thought he was going to punish her. The problem cleared up when we taught the dog not to go on the furniture by putting a cotton spool under one leg of the couch so that it moved whenever he jumped on top of it. The dog soon learned that the floor was far more comfortable—and the whole uneasy triangle was solved once and for all when the woman moved out, taking the dog with her, and married someone else.

CONSTIPATION

An adult dog can take up to twelve hours to digest a large meal but usually needs far less time. Within a few hours the solid waste portion of the meal, together with any undigested nutrients, will pass into the large intestine or colon, before being excreted as feces. Compared to the stomach and small intestine, the large intestine is fairly inactive; there, digestion is nearly complete, and most essential nutrients have already been absorbed from the watery mixture of food and gastric juices. All that remains is for the large intestine to absorb water from these wastes, for without this crucial recycling, your dog would have to drink great quantities of water to sustain his body processes. Water absorption is a fairly slow process, though, and matter remains in the large intestine for a relatively long time. If too much fluid is removed, such as when the pituitary gland sends out messages through hormones to demand that extra fluid be drawn into the body from whatever source is available to restore or maintain a proper balance—or if the food was too dry to begin with—the result is a hard, compact stool that produces constipation.

The owner of a standard poodle came to us because his dog instead of defecating normally would make several false starts, squatting for a few seconds then getting up and walking off as if the urge had passed. As a result, what should have been a simple ten-minute walk was lengthening into a half hour or longer—a frustrating delay for a man whose time was limited. Besides, the straining to eliminate could cause blood vessels to break in the rectum and around the anus,

causing bleeding and irritation. We suggested that the
man have his poodle checked by a veterinarian. During
palpation of the dog's rectum, the vet noticed that the
residual stool in the animal's colon was a bit hard. Of
course, this symptom and the frequent squattings
pointed directly to ordinary constipation. The owner
confirmed the diagnosis when he admitted that the
poodle's stool usually appeared hard and that the dog
seemed to find it easier to evacuate after fifteen minutes
or so of walking around. (Exercise tends to stimulate
the large intestine.) The vet recommended that the
owner give his pet some mineral oil to soften the feces
and help them pass on through.

Usually we believe in following a veterinarian's advice, but this time we vetoed the suggestion. Mineral
oil can "kidnap" fat-soluble vitamins A, D, E, and K
and prevent their absorption into the bloodstream. In
our opinion, faulty diet and lack of exercise seemed the
likely culprits for the poodle's problem—and in fact,
the costive canine turned out to be eating one of those
highly concentrated dry foods. "High caloric density"
is one dog food manufacturer's term for a product that
packs a maximum of energy and nutrition in a minimum amount of bulk. As a result—or so the claims
run—your dog's digestive tract doesn't have to work as
hard for his daily nourishment. But in this case, the
poodle never could drink enough water to moisten this
highly compacted food properly, and his large intestine
efficiently removed what little moisture the dry food
did absorb.

We prescribed a switch to canned food, as well as a
series of exercises to stimulate the poodle's sluggish
digestion. Within a few weeks, the dog was defecating

promptly and easily, saving his owner time in walking that he could then spend in exercising the dog—a healthy trade-off no matter how you look at it.

Mineral oil is only a temporary solution, as are laxatives, which often hurry food through the digestive tract too quickly for proper nutrient absorption to take place. To cure constipation, it's better to simply give your dog more exercise and more fluid and fiber in his diet. (For more on fiber, see page 134.)

The cause of constipation isn't always internal, however. Lola, another standard poodle who was growing normally (sixteen pounds at four months) hadn't had a bowel movement in one and a half days. Her owners were justifiably worried and, before taking the dog to the vet, asked us to come by. We were quizzing them about Lola's recent diet and any other possible illnesses when we noticed the poodle biting at the base of her tail. We took a closer look, and there was the answer: Lola had yet to be clipped in the classic poodle cut, and some of her last bowel movement had become matted in the long hair around her rectum, effectively sealing off the area. This hair matting is a surprisingly common problem among longer-haired dogs, but is easy to remedy with a wet paper towel and a sharp pair of scissors. The only thing you need to be careful of is not to remove so much hair that the dog looks mangy or unkempt. A dog in the wild probably wouldn't run into such a mundane problem, but then dogs with really long hair don't exist in the wild. Some wild canines have heavy coats they develop as protection against the cold, but long hair (as we understand the term in some domestic breeds like Yorkies) would not be genetically adaptable in a wild dog and so did not evolve there. This type of fur mats, and holds burrs, and also serves as an easy breeding ground for fleas and ticks. The domestic breeds of dogs that exist today are "man-made": breeders or dog fanciers have found certain traits desirable that might have occurred through a genetic quirk, and they have bred for or to intensify that quality. The many kinds of dogs we have today are not bred by natural selection for survival in the wild but rather to fit the whims of people and they survive for that reason.

A male dog who strains to defecate may also be suffering from an inflamed prostate gland, which can also cause difficult urination and possibly a greenish or yellowish discharge from the penis. If, while your dog is defecating, a lump or swelling appears on either side of the anus, this indicates a hernia, which requires surgery.

If you see your dog dragging his rear end along the ground, it's not a sign of itching or hemorrhoids but a signal that his anal scent glands are clogged. Two glands, one on either side of the anus, release a distinctive scent whenever the dog defecates. (Dogs immediately sniff under each other's tails to become acquainted with a newcomer's characteristic odor.) You can press out the fluid gently when bathing or brushing your dog, but it's best to encourage the glands to empty naturally by adding bulk to his diet in the form of rice, cooked grain, or other vegetable matter.

Numerous studies have proven that animals enjoy better health when their diets have a certain amount of volume provided by indigestible, but biologically inert, cellulose. The main component of the cell in most vegetables and grains, cellulose cannot be fermented by bacteria and helps ensure a slower, more gradual absorption of sugars by the small intestine. More important, it gives the stools both bulk and texture, which makes them pass along more quickly. And, on the whole, it's best for these wastes not to linger in the colon too long. The large intestine teems with bacteria, most neither helpful nor harmful, though a few do synthesize certain vitamins and other substances useful to the body. But if more nutrients reach the large intestine without being absorbed, there is a greater chance that these bacteria will release toxins and other by-products that can be absorbed into the body.

This is the main argument for high-fiber diets for man and beast alike—to stimulate the colon to move wastes along before too much fermentation can occur. But the high-fiber diet appropriate for humans is not appropriate for dogs, who can't digest lettuce, other salad greens, or tomatoes. For them, well-cooked cereals and protein-rich legumes are fine sources of fiber, but too much of this bulk can have a strong laxative effect. You have to be sure your dog's small intestine has time to digest the food on its way through his system. Basically, the texture of the fiber is more important than its sheer quantity. If it is finely powdered, grain has little or no effect on a dog's intestines; but coarsely ground, it is extremely purgative. Yet if it is served to a dog without being cooked or given any other treatment, grain will simply cause constipation! The fiber you feed your dog shouldn't be a major component of his diet and must be soft and gentle enough not to cause irritation.

THE SEARCH FOR THE PERFECT STOOL

Too many owners try to second-guess the veterinarian by wondering how their dogs' feces should look. A loose stool does *not* indicate diarrhea; in fact, it's healthier for the dog not to have to pass dry, highly compacted waste. If your dog's stools are an odd pink or purplish color, that's most likely food dye from whatever commercial product he's eating. Genuine warning signs include flecks of blood, usually caused by rough food in the colon. Excess mucus can result from intestinal inflammation. Black, tarry feces are the result of internal bleeding in the stomach or small intestine, where the blood has had time to be partly digested. Your vet will want to confirm the diagnosis, of course, so deposit a stool sample in a glass jar or plastic bag. If there's going to be a lengthy delay in getting it to the vet, seal the container tightly and put it in the refrigerator.

DIARRHEA

If wastes pass through the colon too quickly for their water content to be absorbed, the result is diarrhea. Diet changes, a tidbit gleaned from the garbage can, or a dose of milk or other undigestible substance can all result in runny, watery stools. Worse, a dog with diarrhea has to relieve himself repeatedly and often—and usually won't be able to get outside in time.

Most such bouts cease as soon as the large intestine manages to expel the offending substance. But if the intestine itself is irritated or inflamed, diarrhea can continue. And if it keeps on for more than twelve hours, it can cause significant loss of fluid, along with water-soluble minerals and all-important B vitamins. If diarrhea is severe enough, a small dog can die of dehydration within twenty-four hours.

The reason is simple: if the large intestine cannot absorb water, the system is deprived of most of its normal source of fluid. The body of any mammal needs a certain minimum amount of water to help flush wastes (including uric acid, the by-product of protein breakdown) through the kidneys. If these substances aren't removed from the bloodstream, they can quickly build up to toxic levels. Then, in a pinch, the body will take moisture from the protoplasm inside the individual cells. In such a case, the body's fluid balance may be thrown off, leading to an electrolyte imbalance which might throw off the regulating mechanisms of the body and affect vital body functions. There is a balance set up between the fluid inside individual cells and that surrounding them. The fluid surrounding the cells contains sodium and chloride ions; the fluid inside the cells contains magnesium and potassium. A balance between these ions is essential. If the body has to resort to taking fluid from protoplasm inside the individual cells, the result could be disastrous. For example, potassium depletion could result in kidney problems.

The first symptoms of dehydration in man and dog alike are excessive thirst and a dry mouth, because saliva production is inhibited to conserve moisture. One test is to pinch a fold of your dog's skin. Skin with a healthy moisture content swiftly snaps back to its original contour; if the skin is slow to return to normal, dehydration may already be quite serious. But no matter how desperately thirsty your pet may be, don't allow him to gulp water. Even if he doesn't vomit it back up, too much water, drunk too swiftly, can overload his stomach. Set down his water dish, let him drink for about fifteen seconds, and then remove the dish for about twenty minutes to a half hour. Or just drop a few ice cubes in his dish. He'll lick at them eagerly, but the cubes will melt slowly enough that he won't do himself any harm.

To halt canine diarrhea, some experts recommend feeding the animal either Gatorade or applesauce. This is fine if you can tie your dog down and force these substances down his throat—which will probably be necessary, as most dogs won't touch enough of either one to do them any good. We recommend using one of the human antidiarrhea medicines (any of the chalky solutions such as Kaopectate). Give him a dose adjusted to his body size. And if these home remedies don't have a fairly prompt calming effect on the dog's intestines, your vet will have other remedies to prescribe.

Should diarrhea occur along with other symptoms, such as fever, vomiting (which causes even more rapid fluid loss), or bloody feces, don't try to treat the problem at home. See your vet immediately. The cause may be salmonellosis, a bacterial disease that can be thwarted by antibiotics. If your dog's diarrhea seems cyclical, returning every week or so, the cause is most likely to be an infestation of parasitic worms (see Chapter 9).

Until a bout of diarrhea subsides, it's not a bad idea to let your dog's digestive tract calm down by feeding him a gentle diet of chicken, boiled rice, and broth in place of his regular fare. If he has been vomiting and otherwise not digesting what he's eaten, it's important that he take *some* kind of nourishment to ward off malnutrition. Also, wait at least three days before taking your dog on any long walks, or letting him perform any of the exercises detailed in Chapter 9. They are designed not only to stretch your dog's muscles but also to stimulate his entire system—and his digestive tract will quiet down faster if he's allowed plenty of rest.

7

How Feeding Can Make or Break Obedience Training

 Proper feeding is an absolute essential if you want a well-behaved dog. Giving him obedience training depends on your expectations. At one end of the spectrum it can mean teaching a dog to be a well-behaved house pet. At the other end it can mean teaching him to be a champion in terms of the American Kennel Club Obedience Trials. Or, it can mean anything in between.

Our advice is geared to make your dog fit into your life-style. This goes further than, and takes a different approach from, the basic training information given in other training books. We give you the underlying principles to achieving a well-behaved pet. Not only is a dog what he eats in the physical sense. What, when, and how much he eats is the key to controlling his behavior.

It's not possible to train a dog twenty-four hours a day—but during that time, his daily regimen exerts a subliminal message all its own. And it isn't just *when* you feed a dog that has a significant effect on whether he grows to be docile and obedient, but also *how* you feed him. If he's fed on time, walked, and played with on a regular schedule, he knows he can depend on you as his pack leader and has less reason (and fewer opportunities) to challenge your authority. On the other hand, if you aren't aware of how your dog thinks, you can easily teach him an unintentional "lesson."

All too many owners have been misled by dog food commercials that show a number of animals eating from the same bowl. That's a good idea only if you're trying to compose a shot that will look good on the small screen of a TV. In real life, group feeding can lead to either malnutrition or obesity, depending on the size and status of the individual dogs.

In the wild, feeding is never a democratic affair; the pack leaders get to consume the choicest organs and best parts of the carcass. (Among spotted hyenas, females are the dominant pack members and eat much more of the prey than do the submissive males.) This isn't merely a matter of greed, but one of the privileges of being "top dog." By eating more, a pack leader obtains the strength and energy to maintain his status. Likewise, if you have more than one dog in your household, the most dominant animal (if not the male, then usually the oldest and largest) will tend to eat the food of all the others. This is why dogs—especially younger puppies—will eat more when fed in groups than when given food individually: each one is competing against his litter-mates. It's also why fights in a kennel so often break out just before feeding time.

It's up to you, then, to keep the peace and thereby reinforce your position as pack leader. Each dog should have a bowl reserved for his use alone. Most dog food bowls sold at pet stores are wider at the base to keep them from tipping over, but a dog with long, floppy ears may need a narrower and higher sided bowl so that only his muzzle reaches inside. Always select a bowl of pottery or stainless steel: plastic or hard-rubber bowls eventually get scratched in cleaning and can retain sour food odors, which subtly conditions your pet to be alert to the smell of garbage. The very best dog bowls have no tight corners, so that an eager feeder can scrape up every last bit of food and moisture. Since dogs aren't particularly neat, it also makes sense to set a rubber doormat or plastic dish-drainer underneath the bowl, both to keep the food from tracking across the floor under the pressure of a hungry tongue and to catch spills.

Many dogs get wildly enthusiastic when mealtime approaches. Then, when the food arrives, they are rewarded for their unruly behavior. If you don't want a pet whose high spirits automatically translate into leaping and barking, then impose a different lesson. When your dog's motivation (that is, hunger) is keenest, that is the best time to teach him self-control. It may seem dictatorial to make your dog sit and stay while you prepare his food and bring it to him. But that small lesson in obedience and patience can pay enormous dividends. This way, your dog associates obedience with being fed. Later, even when you don't reward him with food, he will be automatically more eager to please you and pay attention to your commands.

On the one hand, dogs should be allowed to eat their meals in peace, and everyone in the family (especially the children) should be taught to respect this. On the other hand, dogs left *entirely* alone when eating can become overly territorial about their food bowls. If your dog ever growls when you approach his food or lay a hand on a toy he's chewing, that's a danger signal. Your dog perceives *himself* as the pack leader. Aggressiveness, like so many other canine bad habits, develops slowly. At first it's growling and territorial urination; if not corrected and stopped there, it will escalate to barking and biting. And so you have to break the habit immediately, by a sharp slap and a firm no!

But it's even easier to forestall such a reaction in the first place. Every so often, from the time your dog is a young puppy, have every human member of the household take his bowl away from him while he's eating. Don't tease, and don't do it more than once a day. Simply remove the bowl briefly, add some water or a pinch of the "flavor supplements" discussed in Chapter 10, and return the food to him immediately. This way, he learns not to be possessive of his food—and by extension other objects such as bones, balls, and toys. It also teaches him to trust you. By his getting it back right away, he learns that he doesn't have to be aggressive or defensive. So you can also trust him. And if you return the food with enhanced scent or flavor, he learns that whatever you do benefits him in the long run.

Many dogs (particularly older ones) will leave food in their bowls, perhaps returning to it later. This is both unsanitary in hot weather and a step in the direction of self-feeding. Every dog should have a time limit for finishing a meal. After about thirty minutes, a healthy animal will have eaten as much as he really wants. At that point, remove the bowl, even if he's still picking at it. Throw away the leftovers, then rinse the bowl thoroughly and dry it, putting it back where he can see and smell it. Since the washing removes the odor of the food, this is an emphatic signal that mealtime is over (as well as a means of keeping the bowl clean). If no treats or supplements come his way until his next regular mealtime—usually breakfast—he will learn not to dawdle. Again, it's important to reinforce the point that *you* provide the food and that it's up to your dog to fit himself to that schedule.

A friend of ours who read an early version of this chapter complained that our methods sound a bit "militaristic," as if we expected dogs to behave like cadets at a service academy. Well, in a sense, we do—because that's *exactly* how feral dogs behave. In the wild, the social rules governing a pack are as rigid as any army; in fact, a pack *is* an army of four-legged soldiers. A dog is instinctively bred to accept and *expect* strict discipline. And if he doesn't get it, he begins to impose discipline of his own, such as when *you* sit down to dinner.

BEGGING AND HOW TO STOP IT

The pet dog who doesn't finish his dinner may have a very good reason for doing so—and it's generally one that you've provided, however unwittingly. Are you giving him treats or scraps from the table to tempt his appetite? Perhaps even a midnight snack because you feel sorry for him or like to share your own snack? Congratulations! You've just rewarded your dog for not finishing his meal. *Biologically,* one little piece of bologna may not do him any harm. But it will have pretty dismal effects on whatever discipline you're trying to instill in him. Simply because your dog is so very interested in food, the ways in which you feed him can be crucial to his behavior. And if you aren't *intentionally* sending him a message in the way you feed him treats, then the dog is probably jumping to conclusions that you never intended to convey.

Don't try to buy your dog's love with the foods he likes best. Instead give him what he needs. Quite often a dog *won't* prefer your food to his. In fact, you'll see him begging for foods that you both know he doesn't like—lettuce or radishes, for example. The reason, once again, is dominance. You're his pack leader. Therefore, whatever you're eating must be good to eat; and your dog will assume that, no matter how many times he's been proven wrong. Besides, by sharing your food, he raises his status in the household pack by several notches. So, by giving in to a dog who begs at the table, you are abdicating your position as pack leader. Worse yet, you are making what *he* interprets as a submissive gesture—for in canine body language, a stare is meant as aggressive behavior, a challenge. In other words, those "sad eyes" are basically trying to stare you down, to break your will. And when you give in, your dog has trained you!

Some owners actually prefer to have their dogs snap up crumbs and scraps. But it's a rare dog who's content with what accidentally falls his way. Either some soft-hearted family member will start slipping extra morsels his way or he'll begin active begging. And because a dog makes such rapid associations with *anything* relative to food, your pet can develop a full-blown habit literally before you realize it. You needn't be a behavioral psychologist to instill a Pavlovian reaction; feed your dog from the table just once, and presto! The next time you sit down for dinner, his gastric juices will start flowing and he'll be back ready for more.

The dog who is accustomed to being fed every time he begs is the hardest to retrain, especially if he's used to whining to get his way. One veterinarian suggests that you "cut out the treats slowly so that the dog doesn't feel suddenly deprived." That's excellent advice if you want to break your pet of the habit sometime in the fall of 1994. If he's not behaving the way you want him to, why reward him at all?

For a dog, there is simply no such thing as an occasional treat. Once-a-week rewards are more than enough to keep the habit going—nothing ventured, nothing gained! It may help you to know that in the wild, a begging animal is driven off by the pack leader, who growls and bares his teeth. The best way for *you* to stop a begger is to go cold turkey, giving him no food at all except at his appointed mealtimes. And if he does so much as ask, "growl" by sending him out of the room.

But won't your dog feel deprived then? Not if you play what we call the "dumb human" routine. Next time he comes over, whining and wagging his tail, pretend you don't know what he's after. Instead of food, give him a pat on the side—"Good dog!"—or a scratch behind the ears, not the lavish, extravagant praise he'd earn for performing a command properly, but just plain old garden-variety affection. Do this consistently, and you'll have switched your dog's responses within a very short time. He'll be rewarded, but in a way he didn't expect; and his instincts will have been diverted from trying to obtain extra chow to obtaining your approval.

Odor is a prime factor in triggering your dog's interest in eating; but it's the natural smell of the actual food, not the aromas of your cooking, that'll really grab his attention. If your pet hangs around while you prepare meals, it's not because he appreciates the smells of your gourmet concoction wafting from the oven. Chances are his nose is sensitive enough to pick up the scent of the "raw" food up there (if out of sight) on the kitchen counter—and particularly meats. (But then, sight is a secondary sense to a hungry dog.) Should you accidentally drop a morsel on the floor, notice how your dog will *hear* it fall. Then when he comes over to find it, he will be sniffing frantically, sweeping his head from side to side, rather than trying to find it by sight.

Scraps from your plate are not the most nourishing fare for your dog. But if you're at all like us, you probably feel guilty about eating good, hearty meals every day while your dog gets the same old stuff every evening. If so, you might want to adopt a ritual we developed in our family: every night, we save just a few tiny morsels of our own dinner and—after we're all through and the dishes are cleared away—we call the dogs in and give each one just a taste and no more. Everybody feels good this way.

Over the months, this practice has taught us that you can reduce the amount of food to practically nothing without reducing your dog's apparent pleasure one bit. And certainly the sense of love and sharing is nearly as strong as if you handed over the whole roast beef. Too, since dogs are just as happy with a thimbleful as they are with an entire plate, you can get a bit more adventurous and offer them tidbits that might not be good for them in any quantity. Meat is a natural, of course, but most dogs will accept a tiny piece of celery or carrot too, especially if it's been sitting in sauce or gravy. If your pet turns down the offer, too bad—that's his decision, and you shouldn't feel rejected. But don't give him a selection of other tidbits if he turns the first one down.

A warning, though: such tokens of your esteem are *only* for the perfectly behaved dog who's at his ideal weight, who does not beg from the table *ever*. If you give your dog treats at all, always restrict them to one period during the day—again, such as after dinner. If a dog is fed too often, he'll come to understand that food can arrive anytime, from morning to night, and he'll be hanging around all day in anticipation of an extra. (Some dogs are amazingly good at begging by just *being* there, at your feet, by your chair, or at the side of the kitchen counter.) if your dog does begin anticipating in this way, break him of the habit by serving the treat in his food bowl, just as if it were a regular meal: in other words, he never gets food from you *directly*, only through his bowl.

In short, never give your pet extras unless you intend to keep on giving him extras. And be sure to do so in such small amounts (and long enough after his regular dinner) that he can't possibly assume that they're a substitute for his regular meals. This time lag is especially important, because otherwise a dog can easily assume that treats are a form of glorified dessert, a continuation of mealtime; a signal that you're only kidding when you take his bowl away after the half-hour time limit is up. Otherwise, your dog will eat less of the dinner you've taken some trouble to select and measure for him; he knows that it's all just a game, that his *real* meal is coming later when you and your family sit down to dinner.

Remember the crucial rule of dog feeding: *whenever you feed a dog, you are rewarding him for whatever he was doing in the past two minutes.* If you don't like the way he's behaving, the answer is painfully obvious—withhold any food until he is behaving well. Thus you shouldn't tolerate barking or leaping before his regular mealtime, nor should you serve any treats *during* your own dinner. Unless your dog understands that nothing will be coming his way until after you get up from the dinner table, he'll take any handout as an engraved invitation for begging. It's best to take scraps into the kitchen, scrape them into his bowl—and have him sit and wait until you serve them to him.

If we seem to have taken a lot of space on this seemingly simple procedure, it's because this is essentially a miniature training session. By having to wait while you clear the table, your dog learns that there's no point in rushing things. He'll see that patience—calm, docile behavior—gets him what he wants. If he sits and stays while you prepare the extras in his bowl, he'll be twice as prompt to obey those same commands at other times as well.

Of course, your dog may be perfectly behaved as far as begging is concerned, but still go into business for himself by stealing food off a coffee table or by jumping up and putting his front paws on the kitchen counter. He'll be much better off if you teach him that he's not allowed to eat anything that you don't give him personally, either in his bowl or from your hand. Start when he's a puppy. If he goes for anything that's verboten, tell him no—and before he's six months old, set up a "cookie test."

Quietly, and without any theatrics, place a cookie, biscuit, or other morsel either on the floor or on a low table, well within your dog's reach. Or seem to absent-mindedly drop a piece of cheese or other tidbit on the floor. (This exercise works best with something that's highly scented, which he can locate easily and which he'll find particularly attractive.) When he goes near it, reprimand him sharply or fling a magazine at him from across the room.

Here's the tricky part. The dog should *not* be allowed to eat the morsel. If so, he'll get mixed signals—the reprimand from you, but a tacit reward when he gobbles down the meat. This isn't entrapment, it's just an important lesson that unattended food is off limits.

After a few trials, your dog is certain to leave food alone—while you're around, that is. This doesn't mean that you can leave a roast out to defrost and expect an unattended dog to resist temptation all day long while you're off at work. What it *does* mean is that you can host a cocktail party without risking half the canapés and walk your dog down the street without his nosing compulsively into every garbage can along the curb. Obviously, it's vital that every member of the household agree to abide by the same rules. If there's even one soft heart among you, your dog will quickly seek out that person and devote all his energies to breaking down that person's resolve. And all too often, children (and sometimes a quarreling married couple) will offer a dog treats simply to win the animal's attention or favor.

This leads to a more difficult diplomatic issue: how you deal with others who want to feed your dog.

THE GUEST DILEMMA

Not all your neighbors, relatives, or guests will have read this book. Many still believe the old misconception that the way to make friends with a dog is to feed him—in fact, one veterinarian who should know better has written that "household guests should . . . let the puppy come to them—encouraging him, perhaps, with tempting food treats." Still other people insist that feeding a dog will calm him down. Well, it's true that a dog who's leaping, wagging his tail, and otherwise putting on a show will quiet down once you hand him food—for as long as it takes him to swallow it. And a dog who's just been fed a heavy meal will of course act lazy and relaxed, because he's digesting and a great deal of his blood supply is being directed to his stomach and intestines.

Remember that when company comes—*especially* when company comes—you are still in charge of your dog. It's not fair to him to relax the rules at certain times and then revert to strict discipline. Humans can easily understand situational ethics, but a dog cannot possibly understand why rules should be flexible. To him, every rule that *can* be broken, will be—and consistently, and on a daily basis!

If you have taught your dog not to beg at the table, as you should have, his good behavior can be ruined if just one guest slips him a morsel. Thereafter, even a dog who knows the rules perfectly will go begging to strangers who *don't* know the local rules. The easiest way to prevent this is to send your dog out of the room when you are serving food to visitors. (Ideally, let him go to wherever he sleeps; this is not punishment but preventive confinement.) *Definitely* send him out of the room if you notice him begging from guests. If you do this quickly and quietly enough, your company will never notice the dog's absence. Later, go to your dog and give him plenty of attention; and certainly bring him back in when the eatables are cleared away. In this manner, he'll know that he can always count on getting *your* affection, *your* approval, and doesn't need to court food and caresses from company.

OTHER FREE-LANCE FEEDERS

Even though neighbors may think they're doing your dog a favor, it's better that you teach him never to accept food from strangers. Professional dognappers regularly entice their victims with food rewards; and more than one owner we know has lost a dog to poisoned food deliberately handed out by unknown parties. Nor do you want your pet to perceive every passing stranger as a possible source of nourishment, because you have no control over how nourishing those tidbits may be.

Our weimaraner Plum once broke out with acnelike bumps all over his head. The vet ran a series of allergy tests on him, to no avail. Could it be the household cleaning solvents we were using? We changed brands, but there seemed to be no correlation. Plum's pimples would recur every so often, seemingly at random, and then clear up by themselves after a few days. The condition wasn't so much serious as it was annoyingly baffling.

The condition came and went over a period of months, which gave us plenty of time to eliminate all the variables and watch for any deviations in his daily routine. Eventually, we discovered that the outbreaks occurred only after the owner of the corner delicatessen gave Plum a certain kind of salami. We asked the kindly man to please hold the salami and give Plum only cheese. The pimples never appeared again.

Another dog owner in our building let his pet accept snacks from the same delicatessen owner. It wasn't long before his dog would run out of the apartment every morning and, rather than relieve himself as he should have, tug at his leash and head off in the direction of the corner store. This meant that the owner had to walk the dog *after* his trip to the deli—and so had to carry his hot morning coffee-to-go the whole way, rather than making the delicatessen his last stop before he went back to the apartment house. But this was a comparatively minor problem; soon the dog was straining at the leash, eager for a trip to the deli *whenever* his owner took the animal outside.

The last straw dropped one afternoon when the dog slipped his leash in the park and vanished. A tag on his collar bore the owner's address and phone number, so the man stayed home from work that day, waiting by the telephone. Finally it rang. It was, of course, the deli owner down the street, saying that the dog was sitting happily by the cash register, and would his owner please come and get him.

Stopping the feeding was the only solution. To effect this, unfortunately, the dog's owner had to stop visiting the delicatessen entirely. Having fed the dog for so long, the proprietor complained that it "wasn't fair" to the dog and couldn't understand why the animal had to be deprived of the treats he obviously loved so much.

Yet another of our clients' dogs got into a habit of accepting food from a grandmother who lived down the hall. The elderly woman would ring the owner's doorbell and ask whether it would be all right to give his dog some chicken—or ham, or roast beef, or wiener schnitzel—left over from a family gathering. The owner, knowing this woman was a superb cook, had no objections. But soon his dog was barking in wild enthusiasm and flinging himself at the door whenever the bell rang.

This was a Pavlovian reaction in spades: the dog had made an association between the doorbell and getting fed. (Interestingly, the dog totally ignored the woman when he passed her in the hall or on the street!) We suggested that the owner dampen the reaction, as the behavioral psychologists would say, by eliminating the reward. And so the feedings of leftovers stopped, and— at the owner's request—the grandmother continued to ring the doorbell, but with nothing to offer the dog. But as we anticipated, this food-related habit took far longer to break than it did to establish; and even today, the dog occasionally overreacts to the sound of the doorbell.

Because dogs are so very good at catching on to schedules, your pet can easily figure out the neighbor's daily rounds—and be there, friendly and waggly for his daily handout. But, naturally, neighbors who think they're being kind and nice will be highly insulted when you politely ask that they not feed your dog. It's as if their treats weren't good enough for him (which of course, they aren't!).

It never hurts to use "doctor's orders" as an excuse. Explain that your veterinarian has forbidden your pet any but prescription fare. Most people can relate to that. They'll say, "*awwww, the poor dog,*" and there the issue will end. If you want your dog to avoid treats from other strangers, run an extension of the "cookie test," by having friends offer the dog treats while you reprimand him—and again, *without* letting him gobble down the morsels in question. Then when *you* offer him a treat, let him have it, and praise him, so he understands the difference and is doubly rewarded.

If you *do* want your dog to accept food from certain strangers, okay, but be sure he gets your permission first. When the favored guest holds out the morsel, have your dog sit and stay. Then your "okay" releases the animal from your command and lets him claim the tidbit as a reward. Still, the very best way to avoid canine behavior problems and human hurt feelings is not to allow any treats to begin with. What your dog has never had, he'll never miss.

HOW YOUR DOG LEARNS: FOOD VS. APPROVAL

When we talk about how food and behavior are interrelated, many people assume we're thinking of food rewards—biscuits or other treats given to a dog when he learns a new command. Since a dog is so very strongly motivated by food, doesn't it make sense to use such rewards as an aid to training? Yes and no—

and here's where our advice departs from that of a number of other trainers.

You have to keep in mind that a dog does not as much reason as he makes *associations*. That's why, for example, he'll be ready for his meal at the same time each day; and why the dogs we just discussed developed such strong attachments to doorbells and delicatessens. In both cases, food was not so much a reward as it was an association; which in turn became an obsession—the dogs' minds were on nothing else. And this, very simply, is why we don't advise you to use food rewards in obedience training. It's too easy for your dog to literally forget everything you've taught him when his whole focus is on the treat or dog biscuit waiting in your pocket.

Because your dog makes food associations so readily, it's better to use treats to condition him to *situations*. Sleepy, our five-pound Maltese, was small enough to travel as carry-on luggage in the passenger compartment of an airplane. But at the start, the changes in air pressure bothered him so much that he hated flying and would whine and complain when we put him in his traveling case. Thereafter, we always took him on lunch and dinner flights and fed him small scraps of meat from our own meals; then, he actually looked forward to getting into his airline case. (If you're going to break the rules, do so under circumstances that your pet can't possibly associate with home. Since we fed him from our plates *only* while aboard an aircraft, there was no question of Sleepy's starting to beg once we got back down to earth.)

But when you're trying to get your dog to learn specific commands, bribery of this sort is not the best way to do it. In fact, it often leads to breakdowns in obedience, because *eventually* you're going to want your dog to heed you simply because you say so and not because you're going to reward him with a bite to eat. For this reason, food-reward training is too often temporary; when the promised reward fails to materialize, so does the training. Also, a dog who's just eaten may well decide that doing exactly as he pleases is more enjoyable than sticking around to earn whatever little tidbit you have for him. Essentially, offering a food bribe is a sign of weakness on your part—and in dog training, weakness is fatal.

But if obedience shouldn't be based on the pleasure principle, how *do* you get a dog to obey? Simply by asking him. As long as your dog looks upon you as his pack leader, he'll be more than sufficiently motivated to want to please you. In fact, he'll even try to imitate you in ways you're not immediately aware of—as one of our clients discovered the hard way.

A woman called us to say that her son's thirty-pound beagle had developed a chewing problem. At first, we assumed this was simply another case of the wrong kind of food. But after the diet changes we recommended, the beagle was still chewing the boy's pencils and eyeglasses; already, the mother had had to replace three sets of frames, which was getting expensive. But what made this instance even stranger was that those were the *only* objects that the beagle was chewing.

We figured it was a salt deficiency; the boy's earpieces must have had a bit of sweat on them, and certainly the pencils would have his perspiration on them too. In mounting frustration, we sent the dog to the vet for a full checkup to see if the animal had worms or perhaps a urinary problem. But no, all the tests came back negative. Was the beagle eating too much? No, he kept up his chewing even after his rations were cut in half.

Then we visited the client's home one weekday afternoon. Their son was sitting in the living room doing his homework, absent-mindedly chewing on a pencil. After a few questions, it became clear that only the boy walked and fed the dog. And the beagle did his chewing *only* when in the boy's room, where he chewed the same items his master did—pencils and eyeglasses! This was simply a case of copycat (copydog?) chewing: noticing that his pack leader indulged in a certain behavior, the beagle simply followed it.

In a well-trained dog, this kind of emulation is common, even desirable. If you want your dog to heel, for example, it'll be much easier if he's trying to imitate your pace. Basically, then, as long as your dog sees you as pack leader, he'll want to follow your lead as best he can. (Again, this explains why dogs beg for food they don't like.) So when training a dog at the outset, understand that you're molding his will to yours and you're setting an example. In order to do so, you have to demonstrate leadership and strength of will. *Don't* ever give a dog a choice about obeying you; he'll learn best by "body English"—by being *shown* exactly what you want of him—and by repetition.

Rarely, if ever, is a dog forced to use logic. Instead, he'll simply associate one word with a given behavior—and then take your praise to mean that he's gotten it straight. So for the simplest and most effective lessons, just show your dog exactly what you want and make him feel good about obeying. Since he's genetically programmed to follow his pack leader, he'll look to you as a source of security—someone who will not only feed but protect and approve of him. Therefore, approval and love are really the only rewards you need to extend. Simply get your dog to do the same thing over and over, on different days and under different circumstances and distractions, until it becomes enough of an ingrained habit to take care of itself. That is, a given command should *always* elicit the same response, with no variations. To reinforce a lesson, it helps to have different family members feed the dog every so often and then later, give him his commands, thus assuring that he'll obey them too and not just the individual who feeds him most frequently.

PICKING UP FOOD AND GARBAGE IN THE STREET

Eating spoiled refuse can give a dog food poisoning, gastric torsion, and diarrhea. Rancid fat is a particular problem, since it acts as an "antivitamin," destroying fat-soluble vitamins A and E, as well as some of the essential fatty acids. Extended lack of these micronutrients can lead to hair loss, skin problems, bad appetite, and even death.

But if you need a really good reason to keep your dog out of the garbage, consider pancreatitis. When a dog eats too much of the wrong kinds of food, the pancreas can become so overstimulated that it manufactures extra amounts of a protein-splitting enzyme. Normally this enzyme is stored in an inactive form until secreted into the small intestine. When excess is produced, however, the enzyme can become active while still in the pancreas and begin digesting the protein cells that form the pancreas. The disease most frequently strikes older female dogs who happen to be obese as well (indicating a long history of overeating, with accompanied overstimulation of the digestive tract). The dog in question usually gets an attack of pancreatitis not long after an eating binge. Symptoms include vomiting (and therefore, thirst), weakness, a staggering gait, and a sudden and dramatic refusal to eat. The dog will usually yelp or whine when the abdomen is palpated. Because the pancreas is sore and inflamed, the dog will often lie down and stretch out, trying to take the pressure off the painful organ and obtain more comfort. Tests by a veterinarian often disclose that the pancreas is pumping digestive enzymes directly into the bloodstream, which has nasty implications for the rest of the animal's body.

Dr. Richard H. Pitcairn, a veterinarian who has several ideas on how to treat this disease by diet as well as prescribed medication, believes that pancreatitis crops up most frequently in dogs who have suffered physical and emotional stress and have been fed a diet rich in sugars and fats. It's best, clearly, to forestall the disease in the first place. If your dog is eating a sensible diet low in fats and carbohydrates, he'll be less vulnerable—as long as you keep him out of the garbage.

8

Exercise the Safe and Noncompetitive Way

Owners often misperceive their dogs as highly physical creatures who need nonstop activity. One woman we know used to run her puppy, Paddy, morning and night, have him jump hurdles, and then allow him a half-hour romp with a neighbor's dogs—so that he would "grow up physically fit," as she put it. One day the dog sprained a muscle in his hind leg during one of his marathon workouts. He spent the next six weeks convalescing without any exercise. At five and a half months, Paddy was still a puppy and wasn't fully physically developed. His joints and musculature weren't strong enough for the type of wild, rigorous exercise his owner was putting him through. She should have built her dog up gradually with controlled exercise. Instead, she allowed her dog to run wild as though he were playing a no-rules, no-time-limit rugby match, where a player isn't allowed to withdraw until he's injured and the game ends when every player has fallen down in exhaustion.

Rushing and pushing a youngster beyond his physical abilities and allowing him to run wild is counterproductive. The case of the woman whose pup sprained a muscle because of the excessive regimen she put him through is an example of this. She thought she was doing the right thing, but actually all she did was retard her pup's development. During his six-week convalescence when the dog had no exercise at all, he lost out on much needed activity. More than that, his muscles atrophied and didn't develop as they would have normally. When she started exercising him again, we had to work out a rehabilitation program to get him in shape. Then we laid out a moderate controlled-exercise program that he could follow safely for the rest of his life.

A healthy workout for your dog doesn't necessarily mean the same thing it does for you. Nautilus machines and Universal gym equipment are intended mainly for looks—to build up or tone muscles and help shape the human body. Your dog's muscles, by contrast, are already as developed as they're going to get. For him, exercise needn't be a strenuous, "no pain, no gain" activity—in fact, overextending him will only lead to injuries and veterinary bills.

What he needs are not muscle-building exercises but what are known as aerobics, running and jumping that make him use his lungs and heart and keep his circulatory system working at peak efficiency. And in fact, that's more or less the sort of exercise he'd get in the wild, in the course of stalking and chasing his prey. What you want to give your dog, then, is a series of exercises that put *all* his muscle groups into play—and which he can perform:

1. *regularly*—at least three or four times a week;
2. *safely*—given his age, present level of fitness, and body structure;
3. *enjoyably*—if these exercises aren't fun for you both, one of you will soon stop doing them;
4. *briefly*—for no more than an hour at a stretch; and
5. *restrainedly*—exercising should also act as a reinforcement to or as a means of obedience training.

For a dog, good exercise is like flooring the accelerator in a car: all his body systems, metabolism included, move into high gear. But a dog, just like an automobile, is better off with a smooth, steady pace than with jackrabbit starts. Regular *light* exercise does more good than any sudden sporadic marathons of activity. Remember, too, that a small lapdog seldom needs as much exercise as a larger, longer-legged breed. One owner of a fifteen pound shitzsu asked us for the name of a good dog walker, so that little Swifty could be walked "briskly" for a couple of hours each day: "She just doesn't get enough exercise when I take her around the block." But this woman lived in a fifteen-room Park Avenue duplex. Little Swifty, who was quite active, ran about the apartment all day, up and down stairs, and was allowed to jump up onto all the furniture. For a dog her size, she was getting plenty of exercise in just making her daily rounds. If the shitzsu's owner had put herself through a comparable daily regimen, she would have soon been in good enough shape for the Olympics.

To a great extent, the ideal exercises for your individual dog will be dictated by his age and body structure. Long-backed dachshunds, for example, should not be encouraged to jump or sit up, nor should a dog with possible hip dysplasia. If you have any doubts as to what's safe for your particular dog, check with your vet. It's particularly important to go easy when exercising young puppies whose bones, muscles, and tendons are still growing. You'll notice that very young dogs nap frequently, and many experts now believe that these rest periods are when some of the body's most vigorous growth actually takes place.

In any case, it's known that puppies who are overworked at an early age can develop enlarged hearts that can cause problems in later life. Human athletes are careful to warm up with calisthenics, and you should "warm up" your puppy with similar stressless exercises during his first ten months of life. He'll need lots of gentle activity, in brief periods that allow for rest and even sleep right afterward. Hold off any really strenuous running and jumping until he's nearly full grown. (Of course, a healthy puppy will want to tear around and push his body to the limit, so you have to set the pace in that regard.)

Many owners feel that during a dog's all-too-brief puppyhood he should be allowed to run free with other dogs. One client asked us if we could recommend a canine "play group" for her Akita puppy, who already weighed twenty-five pounds at three months. We had to say we knew of no such play school for dogs, adding that *she* was really the best playmate her dog could possibly have. Certainly it's true that children need to play with other children so that they can learn how to get along with others. But it is *not* important that a puppy learn to play with other dogs. Letting him run free with other animals will simply teach him rudimentary pack behavior. He'll pay far less attention to you and become more attached to his new packmates. Moreover, unsupervised canine "play" can all too often turn into a fight, where two or more dogs gang up and take on the rest of the neighborhood, one by one. Just like a human mob, packs of young dogs will often drift into bad behavior that no one dog would exhibit on his own.

Whatever your pet learns from other dogs, he may have to unlearn back in the confines of your home. You want him to get along with *people*, to be part of your pack, to obey your rules. And this is sure to happen, because a puppy tends to identify quite strongly with whatever creatures he's brought up with, human or otherwise. Our Inches was raised with cats, as were his mother and father, and he always displayed a number of oddly kittenish traits and was especially friendly to cats. Similarly, a dog raised among humans will bond to you.

WALKS

After-Dinner Walks

Most veterinarians will caution you not to exercise a dog right after feeding him. This is certainly true of *strenuous* exercise, which can make a dog throw up and can lead to gastric torsion. On the other hand, a recent study by the Divisions of Nutritional Sciences at Cornell University proved that exercise after eating seems to burn up more calories by raising the body's rate of metabolism.

After eating, many dogs will lie down to digest. And while a sleeping pet will burn up a few calories in just keeping his heart and lungs going, this sluggish behavior only encourages him to put on fat. Thus it does make sense to take your dog for a walk not more than a half hour after his big meal of the day. This very gentle exercise will also stimulate his digestion. Then, after a few hours have gone by, you can put him through a more demanding regimen of activity.

"Reward" Walks

For smaller breeds especially, simply taking a dog outdoors to relieve himself constitutes a certain amount of exercise. But if you rush your pet back indoors as soon as he's done his business, any moderately intelligent dog will soon learn to prolong his outdoor time, by dawdling for as long as possible before he defecates—a strategy that is quite familiar to many a hapless owner. If you find you are suddenly having to walk your dog half a mile before he evacuates, either you have a severely constipated animal or else the dog has trained *you*. Do you have to walk ten blocks before every bowel movement?

Exercise assists but does not *cause* defecation; and a dog doesn't need exercise to loosen his bowels unless he's ill. Therefore, we suggest you practice what we think of as relative confinement—as soon as you go out the door, walk your dog briskly and directly to his familiar spot. Then, until he defecates, walk him in a tight circle or ellipse. If you have a back yard, designate a special toilet area and stand right by him until he goes; only then take him off the leash and let him run free. Once he's through, *then* he can have as long a reward walk as you're willing to give him.

This method assures that your dog learns that prompt defecation will be rewarded by freedom and not punished by a swift return indoors. Moreover, he'll be ready to defecate as soon as he gets outside, so that he can progress to that reward—a habit that will come in very handy on cold, rainy nights. Rain can be one of your worst enemies in housebreaking, but won't be if your dog is trained to go as soon as you take him out of doors.

Any reward walk must be fairly slow-paced; you want to allow your dog to sniff the sidewalk and ground and generally take his time. (If your dog is a male, the inevitable pauses for urination will help him empty his bladder more completely.) To make this mild exercise a bit more strenuous, lead your dog uphill, over the roughest terrain your clothes and shoes will permit. If you live on the fourth and fifth floor of an apartment building, don't take the elevator; it's healthier for you both if you walk up and down the stairs.

The "Exercise" Walk

An "exercise" walk is different from a reward walk in two ways: you needn't wait for the dog to relieve himself (though he often will anyway, stimulated by the smells and activity of moving about), and it can be longer and more strenuous. Studies show that, in humans at least, very brisk walking—that is, a fast pace just short of running that stretches the leg muscles and works up a mild sweat—is most beneficial for the cardiovascular system. Your dog can certainly keep pace with you on a leash, and if he's been taught to heel he can follow along right beside you.

For even more exercise, you can use the method said to have been employed by Amerindians in their cross-country journeys: run for one minute, walk for three, run for another minute, and so forth. For your dog, these brief periods of running will be the equivalent of the bursts of speed he'd put on in the wild while trying to overtake prey. But even during exercise, his training continues; as you're leading him on, he should be heeling at your side and adapting himself to your pace. If he's on a leash, he shouldn't be pulling you along, nor should you have to drag him.

RUNNING

The cheetah, the fastest land animal known, has been clocked at speeds of more than sixty miles per hour—but only for short bursts. That's because a predator doesn't need to be a marathon runner in order to bring down its prey; it needs only to put on brief rushes of speed. Similarly, dogs in the wild do a lot of running, but mainly during a chase. Most of their daily exercise is simply walking—a fact you should take into account when planning your pet's regimen.

Taking your dog on your daily run may not necessarily be in the best interest. Many runners swear that a special feeling of well-being overtakes them after the second mile or so, but no one has ever reported that canines experience a similar long-distance rush—aside from the ordinary exhilaration of having heart and lungs going at full measure. If you must run your dog, don't take him running on hard surfaces. As any veteran jogger will tell you, the best surface to run on is not a sidewalk or paved road but on earth. This is doubly true for your dog who doesn't wear running shoes. Worse, he's not likely to use his most comfortable running gait in his efforts to keep up with you. Constantly having to adjust his stride may give him muscle cramps, and an uneven, desperate gait can easily scrape the pads of his feet against the rough pavement. And since he can outpace you so easily, he's likely to get bored if he must slow himself to your relatively slower pace. We once asked a rabid runner what it was like to have to be matched with a much slower runner. The answer was: not bad for the first mile or so, but after that tedium, leg cramps, and frustration all the way. The same is probably true of your pet. In fact, the pace could be harmful to your dog, especially for one who is out of condition. And unless you're keeping a close eye on your animal (a neat trick, if you're running on that inadvisable hard surface of the road and are watching for traffic), he may tire prematurely and have no way to signal his fatigue.

Some owners reason that since a dog can run faster than a man, he also needs to run *longer* to get his full quota of exercise. Such an owner might narrow the stamina gap by leaping onto a bicycle and leting the dog run along beside him on a leash. One of our clients figured this would be a great way to exercise Elsa, his 100-pound Irish wolfhound. So he pedaled up and down the paths of Central Park with Elsa on a leash behind him, easily keeping up because of her long stride and great size. But all at once, Elsa decided it was time to relieve herself and she stopped short, pulling the leash taut. Her owner was toppled sideways onto the hard pavement and suffered a lacerated knee and a broken arm.

It's not a good idea to make your dog trot alongside your bicycle, especially if you insist on using a leash. A dog will naturally keep as far away from the spinning spokes as he can get and will tend to pull outward to one side, making it harder for you to swerve or steer.

No matter how you run your dog—with you as you run or by your bike as your ride—taking your dog off the leash might not be the ideal answer. If he's well trained enough to follow you implicitly, he will force himself to go at your pace whether or not it is satisfactory for him, even if there's no leash to keep him close by. (It will, of course, stop him from pulling you off your bike.) Moreover, his focus will be on you. And all too often, a dog like this winds up being hit by a car if you are running or riding a bike along a street because he was paying the least attention to surrounding traffic. Therefore, it's up to you to halt at intersections, even when there's no traffic coming and even though it interferes with your rhythm. You have to instill the safeguards and advance thinking that your dog isn't likely to do for himself.

If your dog isn't well trained and you take off his leash, he might simply run off to do what he wants rather than staying with you. Unfortunately, many people assume their dogs will stick with them no matter what. Not so. Dogs are easily distracted by smells or other dogs. These are far more exciting to him than a long, often boring run. He doesn't understand the benefits as you do. And all it takes is a few moments for you and your dog to be parted forever, which happens in all too many cases.

Many people do, however, jog with their dogs and it works out fine because they take care. If you insist on this exercise, always jog in a parklike area where you can be on grass or earth. Jog at a pace that allows your dog to travel at a fast trot or a walk rather than a run. Start your dog off with a half-mile run and build him up to no more than three miles (one and one-half to two for a small dog). Be sure you can see him at all times; if he stops to relieve himself, jog in place and wait until he's ready to go (you may even have to jog in place while cleaning up after him). Don't take him out in really hot weather. Be sure your pet's in good physical condition; check him out with a vet to be sure. And, when you're running, don't forget your dog is your partner; neither one of you is to get involved with other friends—human or canine. If you can jog with your dog this way and keep him under control, the whole procedure can be a great obedience lesson. But it takes work.

At the end of any run, check your dog's feet carefully for cuts and rawness, and don't take him running again until any such lesions are fully healed. The same goes, of course, if the animal is favoring one foot or acting at all lame. A dog who is still limping after the third day should go to the vet for an examination and possibly X rays.

Not everyone has the time for jogging; and not every dog has enough space to roam in throughout the day.

Therefore, if there are limits on your time and space, it only makes sense to give your pet brief romps of fairly active, calorie-burning, heart-pumping play. To our minds, that's one of the chief drawbacks with running as an exercise for canines; it's *merely* an exercise, with no real opportunities for play or for dog-owner interaction.

THE HIDDEN BENEFITS IN CONTROLLED EXERCISE

As we've explained, diet has a preemptive effect on your dog's behavior, helping to avoid problems before they begin. Exercise, on the other hand, is a way of reinforcing previous training. The way you exercise your dog can give him a number of subliminal messages that should make him even more obedient and easier to live with. Whatever exercises you give him should, besides keeping him trim and healthy over the long run, afford you the opportunity to review some basic obedience commands such as "heel," "jump," and "come"—as well as any particular tricks, such as fetching, that you may have taught him. By having to listen to you even while he's enjoying himself, he'll associate obedience with pleasant experiences. And the more closely you supervise his activities outdoors, the better behaved he'll be on his return indoors.

JUMPING

If you don't live near a park or other open space, this exercise can be performed in the house. Because dogs don't need a running start in order to jump fairly high, the area you select can be rather narrow—as long as it's carpeted to afford your pet good traction. Jumping your dog is also the ideal exercise when you're short on time, because in lifting off a dog has to stretch all the major muscles of his legs and chest and has to use some degree of controlled coordination in judging distance and landing.

When Mike, a standard poodle, was hit by a car, a veterinary surgeon had to operate to fix the animal's broken hip. When the fracture had healed, Mike had a limp; the veterinarian prescribed controlled exercise to increase mobility in the hip joint and prevent muscle atrophy, and he asked us to suggest a specific program.

Mike's owner had cleared the basement to use as an exercise area. But when we arrived, we stopped him right away, before the poodle got injured again. The dog could get no traction on the linoleum floor and would slip and slide whenever his owner threw a ball for him to retrieve. (If a dog hurts himself when performing a new exercise, he'll be very reluctant to try it again.) At our suggestion, Mike's owner laid carpeting and had the dog jump a low barrier in the center of the room. Over the weeks, Mike built his muscles back up to normal and loosened the scar tissue to the point where the limp disappeared completely.

Indoors or outside, the best barrier to use is one of the dog-sized hurdles used in obedience trials. The American Kennel Club will mail you a copy of *Obedience Regulations,* which contains instructions on how to build the standard hurdles, but for your purposes a piece of wood between three and twelve inches wide (depending on your dog's size) will do very nicely.

For starting out, a very low board is best. To clear a

low obstacle, dogs will instinctively jump much higher than they have to; and anything above your dog's normal eye level may seem intimidating to him. Fix the board securely to a horizontal base, or secure both ends to the bottom of a doorjamb. Then drape its top edge with a bathtowel, throw rug, or length of burlap so that your dog doesn't scrape his chest or legs on the top edge.

Put your dog on a leash. Step over the board yourself, leading him along after you, and give the command, "jump." Once he obeys you with no coaxing, remove the leash and get him to clear the board with the command alone. Lavish praise after each jump will reward him, increase his self-confidence, and encourage him to do it again. Then you can *slowly* (the next day, or the day after) go on to slightly higher obstacles and other locations, which will keep this exercise interesting and at least a moderate challenge.

Outdoors, the same basic rules apply. The ideal play-and-exercise area is a gently rolling lawn, completely clear of obstacles like lawn furniture, trees, and cars against which your dog can hurt himself; and the area should be enclosed. Take your dog to an open area, like a park, *only* if you are positive that he always comes when called. Also, be sure the object to be jumped has no sharp edges or protrusions; if possible, cushion or "towel" it to prevent injury. (The very sight and smell of the familiar padding will make the object less daunting to your dog.) If possible, try to pick grass or soft earth for your pet's landing strip.

As few as five or six jumps will give a dog a significant workout, so be sure to halt the exercise before he becomes bored or fatigued. In sum, it's best not to have him jump at all if there's the least threat of injury. Never have him try to clear a sharp or ragged object whose contours are hard to judge, such as a gate or picket fence. Nor is jumping good for low-slung, long-backed, or short-legged dogs, such as basset hounds. Great Pyrenees and other oversized, heavy-boned dogs shouldn't be encouraged to jump either; their weight puts too much stress on their joints as they land.

Since your dog will follow your command implicitly, it's up to *you* to make sure he comes to no harm. One spring day, the plate-glass door of our apartment building broke and the jagged shards had to be pried loose from the frame. The replacement glass was slow in coming, and for a week or more we simply stepped over the foot-high aluminum sill on our way out. Inches got into the habit of following us. Then, as his confidence increased, he would run ahead and jump the sill before we got there.

You can guess what happened, and we should have foreseen it ourselves. One sunny day, Inches took his usual running start, leaped, and knocked himself out against a brand-new pane of glass that had been installed the night before. That taught us a lesson: always make sure that an exercise, however innocent it looks at the start, will *stay* safe.

FETCHING AND RETRIEVING

This is one of the best ways to exercise a dog without wearing yourself out. Fetching is an especially good exercise for long-legged, long-snouted dogs like setters, collies, and retrievers.(Pugs and English bulldogs aren't particularly good at this, because the configuration of their jaws makes it hard for them to scoop up objects.) Most dogs will delight in the unexpected bounces of a tennis ball and can learn to nab a hovering Frisbee out of the air.

At the same time, fetching subtly reinforces your "come" command. If he's rewarded by your throwing the object every time he brings it back, he'll be more likely to obey you later as well. Best of all, perhaps, this is one exercise where the dog calls the shots; he'll keep it up as long as he wants to and then simply run off with the thrown object without bringing it back to you.

A small dog is usually able to fetch indoors. If your home features large rooms or long hallways, a larger dog can play inside too. Use a very soft rubber ball, so that an occasional "foul" won't do any damage—but be sure to get it away from your dog as soon as he brings it to you or he'll quickly chew it up and may swallow it.

This brings up a major problem that keeps many dogs from learning to fetch successfully: the texture of the object between their teeth may be even more delightful than the fun of chasing after it. Your dog will tend to prance around proudly, happily teething his new catch before turning it over to you again—if at all. So if you throw one of his chew toys or some other object he's used to playing with, he may not bring it back. Why should he, if it's his to start with? The real secret of teaching a dog to retrieve is to throw an object he associates with *you* and which comes into sight *only* for fetching purposes. When he does surrender whatever he's brought to you, praise him profusely and throw it again *immediately*. The longer you hold onto it, the more your dog is punished, in a sense, for having given it up. But if he positively refuses to bring it back, go get him (*without* calling him), take the object away, and go on to another sport. (You have to be able to catch him easily of course—another good reason why fetching is best taught indoors.)

Fetching is also a good warm-up exercise. Before taking your pet for a long run, throw a stick or ball to make him stretch his muscles. But as always, the secret to any good play is to call it off just before your dog gets tired or loses interest. Keep count, therefore, of how many times he fetches and at what distance. For example, if you hurl a ball twenty-five yards, by the time your dog retrieves it, he'll have run fifty yards. Fling the ball eighteen times, and your dog will have covered more than half a mile.

SWIMMING

If you live near a body of water, your dog can use up in five minutes the same amount of energy he'd expend in half an hour of walking. Retrievers and springer spaniels are particularly fond of the water and will often wade right in. But other dogs may need encouragement. Never throw an animal in to "let him get the feel of it"; this can cause him unnecessary panic and result in a permanent water phobia that's almost impossible to overcome.

As always, body language is the way dogs communicate. For example, when teaching a dog to sit, you must physically push down his hindquarters to show him what you want. The best way to teach a dog to swim, then, is to change into a bathing suit yourself and plunge in. If he sees *you* having fun, he's more likely to follow you—first out of a sense of insecurity of remaining on shore and later out of pure enjoyment. If he needs further coaxing, fit him with his leash and collar and walk him into shallow water.

Most dogs will be fascinated with the push of water against their legs and will soon accept swimming as a natural, instinctive action. Once he's happy in the water, you can throw floating objects for him to fetch—small, easy-to-grasp ones, so that he doesn't choke or swallow water as he tries to get hold of them. Again, remember that swimming takes much more exertion than ordinary exercise, so two or three waterborne fetches are enough of a workout. Exercise should always be fun for you both—never a chore.

For safety's sake, don't ever let your dog swim in a pool without stairs or any other body of water with steep banks where he can't gain easy footing. A dog can tire suddenly, and you can't always predict when. A beach, with sizable breakers, is not for the novice dog, who should be accustomed first to handling the gentle waves on a lake or bay. Once he's gotten a wave in the face a few times, he'll accept it as part of the deal. A few breeds—notably Labradors—will even go on long ocean swims, sometimes chasing seagulls. But most dogs (especially smaller ones) will be much happier kicking around in shallow water where they have more control.

As for that age-old habit dogs have of getting right beside you before they shake themselves dry, they just want to get close to you—and thus feel secure—before drying off. Take it as a compliment!

ANTI-EXERCISES

A few pastimes aren't good for your dog's health or behavior. Many veterinarians recommend tug-of-war as good exercise for puppies and more sedentary dogs. But Dr. John Stump, professor of veterinary anatomy at Purdue University, warns that a game of tug-of-war "conditions the dog to get satisfaction from using his teeth"—which can lead to increased chewing of rugs and furniture. Dr. Stump also points out that when playing with one another, puppies learn not to bite too hard. But with a rope or towel the dog doesn't learn to moderate the pressure of his bite.

Of course it's charming to watch puppies wrestle and tumble with each other—but note that they perform this roughhousing only with each other and never with their mother, who is their pack leader. This kind of playful biting and chasing, then, is exactly the kind of game you *don't* want to play with your dog, because in his eyes it'll lower your status as pack leader. If he beats you at tug-of-war, tag, or some other competitive game, sooner or later he may try to best you in some other way, such as "forgetting" his housebreaking rules. In exercising your dog, you should remain the coach and not descend to becoming a fellow teammate.

Nor should you exercise your pet at the expense of other animals. While walking in the park one afternoon, we saw a young lawyer we know who was encouraging his whippet to chase squirrels. His excuse was that he was only giving his dog some exercise—and the squirrels some harmless exercise too, since the whippet practically never caught them. We asked what happened if the dog *did* catch a squirrel. "Oh, he kills it, of course," the lawyer replied. We reminded him about *Cujo,* Stephen King's bestseller about a once-friendly St. Bernard who contracts rabies after being bitten by a bat, and that squirrels carry rabies too. A single bite from an infected squirrel would be enough to give his whippet the disease. And the likelihood is that, since rabies attacks the nervous system making its victims slower and less coordinated, what the whippet would catch most easily would be a rabid squirrel.

In the animal kingdom, the general rule is, if you get bitten, bite back. And so if you sic your dog on other creatures, you're setting him up for any number of painful wounds, many of which can easily become infected.

THE DANGERS OF CANINE HEATSTROKE

When he's exercising, your dog will usually follow your lead without asking questions. He won't use even what little judgment he has and will have no qualms about overtiring himself. In fact, some older dogs enjoy play so much and are so eager to please their masters that they'll keep pushing themselves until they drop. Let your dog rest whenever he begins to pant rapidly, and let him lie down in the shade where he can cool off.

The 1983 summer heat waves caused nearly a hundred human fatalities, but the toll in dogs was far higher. We actually saw a number of animals collapse. One we recall in particular was a little red-and-white mixed breed that looked something like a Brittany spaniel. His owners and their two children were encouraging the dog to race around Riverside Park despite the 97° heat, "so he could get enough exercise," as they told us later, "and calm down." The dog calmed down all right; he keeled over and couldn't get up. A sympathetic crowd gathered around the family, trying to comfort their stricken pet. But no one seemed to realize the dog was running the equivalent of a high fever and desperately needed to have his body temperature lowered. We got a street vendor to scoop some ice cubes and cold water from the soda cooler in his cart. And wrapping the ice cubes in a bystander's T-shirt, we laid the cool compresses over the dog's body and let him lick at the ice cubes. After the animal seemed somewhat recovered, we suggested the family carry him home.

A dog can sweat only through his feet pads, anus, and tongue. He doesn't have the heat-releasing mechanisms of many other animals. This is why a dog is so susceptible to heatstroke and other heat-related problems. Remember that domestic dogs were bred for traits that people consider desirable either for looks or ability. There was no natural genetically induced adaptability to the natural environment they live in today. People, not nature, controlled them. Even those dogs that are suitable for living in cold climates, such as Siberian huskies and Japanese Akitas, have been transplanted by people to warmer climates.

Good adaptation to heat, however, is not even present in wild dogs. That is why dogs react to heat in what may seem to us to be excessive ways—by panting or digging holes in the earth under shady bushes. You must therefore watch out for your pet in hot weather. Locking your dog in a closed auto can be fatal because a car heats up rapidly—and so does your dog. Exercise raises your dog's metabolism and boosts his temperature, which in turn can lead to heatstroke. If the dog is obese, the problem is even worse, since he then has even more body volume to retain heat.

The owner of a golden cocker spaniel had taught her dog to fetch a rubber ball—an exercise the dog enjoyed so much that the owner kept on with it straight into the hot summer months. One stifling July day, the dog keeled over. This time, we were able to borrow a thermos from a nearby picnicker, soaked a towel in iced tea, and applied it to the cocker's paws and muzzle. Happily, it cooled him down, but his owner couldn't understand why the dog had collapsed in the first place. She had played wth him that way the summer before, she told us, and he hadn't shown any discomfort then. But when she showed us snapshots of the spaniel taken when he was a puppy, we did a double take—the dog who lay panting on the ground was at least ten pounds heavier than he'd been the summer before. It turned out that the woman had switched him to a therapeutic diet and was overfeeding him out of ignorance of how much "medicine" he really needed.

Looking at the photographs and then back at her dog, the woman said she honestly couldn't see any difference. And to be fair to her, it really is difficult to perceive small, day-to-day changes in your pet, no matter how much they eventually add up. In this spaniel's case, his owner cut his daily intake from two cans to one and a quarter, and the dog's weight dropped from about thirty-five to twenty-four pounds inside of four weeks—he lost nearly a third of his body weight!

This story, then, packs a double moral: don't exercise your dog in the heat of the day and keep his weight under control if you intend to keep him active. In hot weather, it's especially beneficial to keep an eager dog on the leash or heeling closely at your side, where he can't overexert himself. Most parks do not have street-level fountains where a thirsty dog can lap water, so it's a good idea to lead your pet to his water dish for a drink before taking him out.

EXERCISE ADDENDA

In cold weather, check your dog's paws when he comes back inside. If he's been out any length of time, he can accumulate packed snow between the pads of his feet—painful in itself, and doubly so if he's picked up any grains of corrosive rock salt, which can cause severe irritation. (As you already know, a dog who licks salt off his paws will develop a raging thirst, seemingly out of nowhere.)

Watching the way your dog plays is just as important as keeping an eye on his appetite and eating habits. If you see him tiring suddenly, check with the vet—premature fatigue can be a result of heartworms or other lung and circulatory problems, as well as obesity.

Regular exercise, you'll soon discover, is a great help in regulating your dog's digestion and elimination—which of course aids in housebreaking and helps forestall obesity. Exercise also helps keep his cardiovascular system in good health. The more efficient your dog's circulation is, the easier it'll be for his blood to absorb the nutrients from the digestive tract and distribute them throughout the body. Similarly, efficient blood flow speeds the removal of wastes and toxins from individual cells for elimination through the kidneys. But ironically, the best part of a controlled exercise regimen is that such an established routine is easiest for *you* to follow. Once taking your dog out for exercise becomes genuinely routine, it'll be no trouble at all for you to find enough time in the day.

It's true that a very active dog will burn up more calories and have a greater appetite. But giving a dog exercise is *not* an automatic excuse to double his rations. Again, consult what the scales say. If your dog is holding to his present weight despite regular workouts, there's no point in feeding him extra. But if he's losing a pound or two, *then* you can increase his daily meal by 5 or 10 percent. Remember that the healthiest animals are slightly underweight, and this is best for his general well-being.

9

Beating the Parasite Problem

 If you accompany your dog on his forays outdoors, it'll be easier to keep him out of long grass and underbrush where he can pick up external parasites such as ticks and fleas—and you can prevent him from eating carrion and small animals that can infect him with internal parasites.

Parasites, internal and external, can wreak havoc with your dog's health and behavior. These creatures feed off your dog and, by extension, on his food. They interfere with the proper utilization of food and cause irritation by digging into and clinging to his body. And they can lead to unacceptable behavior in a dog who is too preoccupied, or too ill, to listen to what he is told to do.

The only solution to health and behavior problems caused by parasites is to get rid of the parasites. Unfortunately, these creatures are numerous and varied, can easily be picked up from many innocent-looking sources, are frequently overlooked as a cause of a problem, mask themselves as other illnesses making diagnosis difficult, and can be difficult to get rid of. But, fortunately, they can easily be avoided and are therefore not all that insidious to well-cared-for dogs living in the clean surroundings of your home.

EXTERNAL PARASITES: TICKS AND FLEAS

If you do find a tick on your dog, just pull it off. Some people claim that a tick's mouthparts can remain embedded in a dog's skin and cause a troublesome infection. Thus, they recommend you touch the tick's body with chloroform, alcohol, or the tip of a burning cigarette to make the tick release its hold. However, these remedies can hurt your dog, and the tick can still remain. If you pull the tick out with tweezers and a tissue, making sure you grasp the head and not the body, the tick should come loose with no trouble. Then touch the area with a 5 percent solution of hydrogen peroxide or alcohol if you're worried about infection.

Although adult ticks can survive many months without food, they are not too much of a problem: this is simply because when they become swollen with blood, they are large enough to be seen, and in a long-haired dog, are easily detected with a comb or brush. Also, ticks lay eggs mainly outdoors, so a tick your dog brings in is not about to breed more ticks on your dog or in the house, as is the case with fleas.

There are some 240 different species of fleas throughout the continental United States, most of which parasitize only one type of animal. *Ctenocephalides canis*, the dog flea, is the main species you need to worry about. Almost every pet dog has fleas at one time or another during his life, yet the flea spends up to 75 percent of its life independent of a host dog.

A female flea will lay her eggs nearly anywhere—on the ground, in the corner of a room, in dust or debris, or in the bedding of her host animals. Her eggs are dry and not sticky; if she does lay them in the fur of a dog, they soon drop off. Two to ten days later, the eggs hatch into wormlike larvae that feed mainly on organic debris, including the droppings of adult fleas—dark, gummy excrement composed largely of undigested blood.

After two moltings, the flea larva spins a cocoon and pupates, waiting in a kind of suspended animation for the tremors that indicate that a possible host animal is passing by. This is why a doghouse or kennel that has been vacant for some months may suddenly be found to be alive with fleas; these are "sleeping beauties" just emerged from their cocoons, aroused from pupation by the footsteps of the new occupants. (In addition, adult fleas can live up to a year.) Since they can cover eight inches in a single leap, it's easy for fleas to grab hold of your dog, burrow down through his fur, and start sucking his blood, thereby providing the excrement that serves as pabulum for the next generation of flea larvae.

Even though your dog's fleas prefer parasitizing a canine, in a pinch they will bite you as well while breeding happily in your rugs, clothing, and bedding. Unfortunately, the tick-and-flea collars that were introduced several years back are not the answer. They contain chemicals proven to cause cancer in humans and can be highly irritating to the eyes and skin (both yours and your dog's). The only reason the FDA approved them in the first place was that they were to be used on animals. Some authorities recommend that you "air" a flea collar for up to forty-eight hours before putting it on an animal, and to watch carefully for rashes and other allergic reactions. But a human can easily pick up the harmful chemicals by patting a dog whose fur has become impregnated with them, and water is likely to cause the poisons to leach out, with possibly serious effects on anyone who pats the animal. The effects on your dog who is exposed to these poisons twenty-four hours a day are significantly greater. Regrettably, the safest ways to control fleas are the old-fashioned ways: prevention and hand-to-hand combat.

The best way to keep fleas in check is to keep your home clean so the eggs and larvae can't take hold, and to keep your dog clean and well-brushed enough so that flea populations don't have a chance to take hold. Give the areas where your dog sleeps special attention when cleaning. Dispose of the dust and dirt promptly, either by burning or in a *sealed* plastic bag in the garbage can. It's particularly important to keep any crannies and nooks around dog houses or where your dog sleeps clean too. (An outdoor dog can be given straw to sleep in, which can be changed every two weeks.)

If your home is heavily infested, you should definitely hire a professional exterminator to eliminate the resident population of adults and larvae. That will give you a chance to narrow the battlefield to those fleas actually residing on your dog. Ask your vet or satisfied pet owners to recommend a safe exterminator. You probably won't get a list of the ingredients used by exterminators so you can check the safety for yourself. But be sure to have the person you hire guarantee that the products he uses are not harmful to pets. Keep your pet—and yourself too—out while, and for at least a few hours after, the job is done. If your exterminator wears a heavy-duty mask, definitely your dog and you should not be in the area breathing in the fumes. Wash or throw away your dog's bedding when he's exterminating to be sure no strong residual chemicals remain. Follow the exterminator's precautionary instructions and use your own common sense.

Many professional dog breeders regularly dip their animals in flea-killer baths. Richard Bradley, a parasitologist at the University of Florida, recommends insecticides containing organophosphates, even though they can be highly toxic and must be used sparingly lest they dry out the dog's skin. To be on the safe side, we recommend you use an ordinary soap or shampoo. Simply making your dog sit in warm water for about fifteen minutes will drown all the fleas below the water line. You can then wash his head and neck with a nontoxic, herbal flea and tick killer available in health food stores. Or you can make your own by boiling one teaspoon of dry or fresh rosemary in one cup of water. Between baths, dust your dog with a safe, organic flea powder made by mashing up dry rosemary with citronella, eucalyptus, pennyroyal, rue, wormwood, and dry brewer's yeast.

It may also help to *feed* the dog brewer's yeast, since there is some evidence that the B vitamins it contains can help repel fleas. Just add one rounded teaspoon to your dog's daily meal. (But don't forget that yeast is very high in calories.) Various other experts and dog breeders advise adding a tablespoon of vinegar daily to your dog's ration of drinking water, or mashing vitamin C, cod liver oil, a clove of fresh garlic, and/or ten milligrams of chelated zinc into the dog's daily food.

Probably your best bet is to use the stronger insecticides recommended by your veterinarian on rugs and around your dog's bedding (which should be washed regularly), while reserving the milder, more natural remedies for the animal himself. Remember, though, that a flea's eggs take up to a week to hatch, so repeated baths and fumigations every two weeks are needed to dispose of succeeding generations. Flea dirt is often the first sign of the coming of fleas. This looks like little black poppy seeds and consists of a mixture of eggs and waste.

It's important to control fleas while their numbers are still manageable. If your dog is heavily infested, sheer loss of blood can lead to anemia. Worse still, fleas serve as an intermediate host for at least one species of tapeworm. Along with organic debris and excreted blood, flea larvae will often consume tapeworm eggs—which they do not digest—and if a dog licks at and swallows an adult flea, the tapeworm eggs develop and begin their life cycle.

INTERNAL PARASITES: WORMS

When out with our dogs in Central Park one day, we crossed leashes with an old friend who was walking Tavish, his Scottish terrier. The dog seemed a bit under the weather, but the owner was even more haggard; his eyes were red and his face was a mask of grief. When we asked him what the matter was, he shook his head. Then, apparently eager to unburden himself, he went on to tell us: "I just discovered my wife's having an affair with her old boyfriend."

Of course we were shocked and surprised. How had he found out? Our friend shook his head sadly. "You told me that a dog can't digest starches unless they're properly cooked, right? Well, just a few minutes ago, Tavish passed some linguine that he hadn't digested. I *hate* linguine, and so does my wife, but her old Italian boyfriend loved the stuff. Back when they lived together, she used to cook it for him all the time, the way he liked it—*al dente*. I've just been away for ten days on business, and that guy must have been over to visit. How else would Tavish get hold of linguine?"

By way of emphasis, our friend showed us the clear "pooper" bag he had just used to collect the terrier's stool. Sure enough, the feces were laced with what looked like strands of linguine—*segmented* linguine. When we saw them, we quickly segregated our dogs from the infected Tavish. We told our friend to worry about his dog and not his wife. The linguine, we explained, was in reality proglottids—the linked body segments of a tapeworm. An adult tapeworm (which is invariably female) consists of a gut and tiny head that attaches to the host's intestinal wall. The segmented "tape" that appears to be the body of the worm is the proglottids, a series of self-contained capsules, produced end to end, each containing male and female sexual organs. As these segments grow and mature, the ones at the end of the chain eventually break loose and—then teeming with fertilized eggs—are passed along with the feces. Any animal that eventually ingests those eggs can be infected. Our friend was ecstatic; he said he was going to buy flowers and run off home to tell his wife. We told him he'd be better off seeing a vet!

Diplydium caninum, the tapeworm spread by fleas, is by far the most likely species for a dog to contact. But he can also pick up the tapeworm *taenia taeniaeformis* from eating infected meat or a rat or mouse already harboring a worm and its proglottids in its digestive tract or encysted in its muscles. The *taenia* species of tapeworm, whose proglottids are shaped like cucumber seeds, usually afflicts dogs in rural areas. It can also infect humans, though rarely if ever do humans pick up worms from dogs.

Most intestinal worms dampen a dog's appetite, but a tapeworm has little or no effect—if anything, it will make the dog want to eat more. An infected dog will sometimes scoot his hindquarters along the ground, as if he were suffering from clogged anal glands, but close examination of his stool will, sooner or later, reveal seedlike proglottids which move with an inchwormlike motion. By comparison, other species of intestinal parasites are relatively easy to treat and eliminate. But to kill a tapeworm's resilient head takes a very strong medication, following an eighteen-hour period during which food is withheld from the dog. Sometimes the canine host must be given medicated enemas to get rid of the tapeworm once and for all.

Folklore has it that feeding a dog candy will cause him to contract worms. In reality, sugary foods will only help nourish whatever worms the dog already has. Animals contract tapeworm (as well as other intestinal parasites) not by eating candy but by consuming raw meat (which folklore insists should be a part of every dog's diet). Rabbit meat is particularly apt to be tainted and should always be cooked thoroughly before being offered to man or beast. Pork is especially likely to harbor the trichina worm, *trichinella spiralis*, which causes trichinosis. This creature was first observed by British surgeons in 1828 in the muscles of human corpses. The reason pork is so risky is that pigs (like rats and mice) have a habit of eating refuse and scavenging in areas where other infected animals have defecated stools containing worm eggs.

Aside from pork and rabbit, the meat from your butcher isn't likely to harbor parasites that can affect you or your dog, but to be on the safe side, never feed the dog meat without cooking it. The same advice about cooking goes for freshwater fish, which can harbor the fearsome giant kidney worm, *dioctophyma renale*. Adult worms measure up to six inches in length and slowly consume the infected host's kidneys. The victim discharges blood and pus and eventually dies of kidney failure or uremic poisoning. This parasite is distributed throughout the world, and its life cycle is almost unbelievably complicated. Eggs are passed through the victim's urine, take six months to mature, and remain viable for at least four years thereafter. But they do not hatch until eaten by a certain kind of worm that parasitizes crayfish. Only if these worms are later eaten by fish does the kidney worm go on to develop into its third and fourth larval stages. The mammals who become the kidney worm's victim become infected by swallowing larvae in raw fish. This is a pretty far-fetched scenario for the average dog owner to worry about, but it is interesting.

Other parasitic worms can lodge in various organs of the body, including the liver, muscle fibers, lungs, brain, and heart. But for the most part, it's the digestive tract where they prefer to make their homes. Contrary to popular myth, intestinal worms do not share a dog's food—if they did, their presence would cause the dog little or no harm. Instead, they usually attach themselves to the mucus lining of the intestine and feed on the dog's blood. You can think of them, then, as internal fleas—and in any quantity, they can be just as debilitating. Initially, worms will cause mild anemia, but sooner or later, their presence begins to irritate the digestive tract and hamper its ability to absorb nutrients. As the intestines become inflamed the dog naturally loses his appetite, which only compounds the likelihood of malnutrition.

We were once tempted to throw in the towel on a bloodhound we'd been trying to train over a six-month period. Originally, her owner had telephoned us because the dog was chewing on household articles as well as herself, and defecating indoors to boot. These problems had begun shortly after he had brought her home, and so we began working with this dog almost from the start. At the outset, we suggested that the owner take one of the dog's stools to the veterinarian to have it checked for worms. She had them, all right—an infestation of roundworms she'd brought with her from the breeder.

The vet gave her an appropriate worming medicine, and we figured the problem was solved. But when the bloodhound kept on chewing and defecating indoors, we sent her back to the vet for a second worming and a third, just to be on the safe side. With his assurance that she was worm-free, we went ahead with her training. Then, a few weeks later, she had another relapse.

After a diet change and appropriate reprimands, the dog would be perfectly well behaved—for a few weeks. Then suddenly her owner would return home to find chewed pillows and clothing and two or three piles of feces on the floor. This cycle went on for months. It was a toss-up which disgusted the owner more—his dog for reverting to her old behavior or us for assuring him repeatedly that the problem was solved.

This dog was a real puzzle to us because she was eating a good, sound, healthy diet. The owner claimed he never gave her any extras and exercised her properly, giving her plenty of opportunities to go outside. Of course, even a well-behaved dog will sometimes break training just to test a master's authority, but this kind of rebellion is less common in females. Moreover, such lapses are usually temporary and easily corrected. Never before had we encountered a dog with such persistent, regular, *total* breakdowns in behavior. It was exactly as if she suffered some kind of brain lesion that periodically shut down her memory system and made her forget everything she'd learned.

Another problem—mild by comparison and easy to overlook—was that the bloodhound never seemed to achieve the good physical condition she should have. She always looked slightly underweight, not by itself a sign of poor health, but at age one she still hadn't attained her full size. Both her parents had been good-sized bloodhounds. Was she the runt of the litter?

We concluded there had to be something seriously wrong with her digestion, since she was displaying all the behavioral and physical symptoms of a diet deficiency. But the vet insisted that he could find nothing wrong and that her lapses were the result of *our* failure to train her properly.

Finally we persuaded the dog's owner to get another opinion, from another veterinarian. He was reluctant, since the vet he'd been seeing had been recommended to him by his own mother. But after the bloodhound started chewing on one of his mother's wedding presents (a rare side chair made by Rhode Island cabinetmaker John Townsend, circa 1770), he agreed. Amazingly, both the new veterinarian and a third tiebreaking vet we hired to give the deciding opinion both declared that the dog still had worms!

What worried us was that the bloodhound was severely malnourished, anemic, and run down—as is usual with long-term worm infestations. And because she had been suffering their effects for well over a year, the treatment had to be vigorous and prolonged. We were worried because all worm medicines are essentially poisons that, ideally, will be rougher on the worms than on the dog. For this reason, many vets will prescribe several light wormings, rather than one heavy dose of medication that may be strong enough to cause side effects and not get all the worms. But happily, proper treatment got rid of the bloodhound's infection, and once her health was restored with dietary supplements, her training lapses became a thing of the past.

Were all her problems the result of that first veterinarian? Not necessarily. We later discovered that her owner had been giving her plenty of time outdoors, letting her sniff around in an area where many other dogs went to relieve themselves. The chances were very good that the dog had reinfected herself repeatedly, even after the vet's treatment had wiped out the original infestation.

This dog was afflicted by roundworms (*toxicara canis* and *ascariasis* spp.), which are a very common problem with young puppies. As a dog grows older, he usually develops antibodies against roundworms. But the stress of pregnancy can weaken a bitch's immunity, so that by the time she is ready to give birth, a previously low-level roundworm infection may have flared up to significant proportions. But a pregnant dog can't be wormed because the necessary medicine can damage her unborn litter. (Therefore, responsible breeders make every effort to have a female wormed *before* she's bred.) Puppies are usually infected before birth, when roundworm larvae in their mother's bloodstream penetrate the placenta. Later, after birth, the puppies can ingest more larvae through her milk. Once in the puppy, worm larvae make their way to the lungs, where the dog coughs them up, then swallows them so that one way or another, they wind up in the dog's intestine.

A puppy with a heavy roundworm infestation will have a distended abdomen and show visible discomfort as a result of intestinal irritation. The coat will be dull (a sign of malnutrition), and the puppy will often suffer from diarrhea and vomiting, often expelling two-to-three-inch worms that curl into a circle (hence the name *round* worm). There are other clues that should alert you to worms: a dog who's eating a good diet, but who still keeps losing weight (or, in the case of a puppy, fails to gain it). The bloodhound we just discussed was a walking textbook of symptoms. Anemia (usually manifesting in lethargy, poor spirits, and emaciation) should make you suspicious. Other prime worm symptoms are diarrhea and flatulence that have no apparent relation to other illnesses or changes in diet. When the worms irritate the dog's small intestine, the dog's system tries to expel them forcibly. Bloody diarrhea is practically a giveaway.

Whipworms *(trichuris vulpis)* infect the colon; afflicted dogs will often worry at themselves (sometimes called "flank-sucking") to distract themselves from the internal discomfort. As when he has other species of worms, the dog may show emaciation, occasional diarrhea, and anemia. A dog who vomits in the morning, on an empty stomach, is often a whipworm victim; the movements of the worms make him queasy and sick to his stomach. And since roundworms pass through the lungs en route to the intestine, heavy infestations of larvae can also cause pneumonia, since his general malnutrition leaves the dog vulnerable to a wide spectrum of infectious diseases.

Obviously, the idea is to get rid of the worms as speedily as possible. But it's important to have the worming supervised by a vet. Even if necessary, worming shouldn't be performed on a very young puppy because the medicine can damage an immature digestive tract. Moreover, too frequent worming can play havoc with a dog's digestion, no matter what his age.

You may have seen advertisements for over-the-counter worm medicines that you're supposed to add to your dog's food once a month. But depending on your dog's size, these fixed dosages may be either too high or too low. Worse, the timing is wrong: roundworm medication is effective against only *adult* worms; and so two or more wormings must be administered, at ten-day intervals, to finish off any larvae that may have matured in the meantime.

Lastly, these medicines are aimed specifically at roundworms but are not at all effective against the other dozen or so species of parasitic worms that a dog can pick up. Having one set of parasites is no guarantee that your dog doesn't have several others. Each species requires its own medication, dosage, and course of treatment. That's why a professional examination of a dog's stool is necessary: not to determine *whether* the dog has worms, but to figure out what kind they are.

Yes, humans can get roundworms too. A few types of worms—including tapeworms, pinworms, and hookworms—also infect people, but owners rarely catch these parasites directly from their dogs. Given the worms' bizarre life cycles, it's nearly impossible. People usually get worms by ingesting worm eggs in uncooked meat or fish or by coming in contact with infected dog feces, which is not likely either, unless you happen to be a small child playing in the soil where dogs have defecated up to several weeks before. A dog's feces break down rather quickly, but worm eggs persist in the soil for a surprisingly long time—and thus dogs (such as that poor bloodhound) can reinfect themselves in a distressingly wide number of ways, from sniffing up worm eggs to simply walking on the ground. (Larvae of the hookworm, *necator americanus* and *ancyclostoma duodeneale,* enter a dog by burrowing through the skin of the pads of his feet. Dogs can also be infected through the bite of a flea or mosquito, or by licking or sniffing an infected animal. But in general, the best form of worm prevention is the "pooper-scooper laws" that require dog owners to clean up after their pets. Besides improving sanitation, these laws help cut down on the transmission of parasites; and the more communities that pass these laws the better.

Fortunately, few worms are able to parasitize more than one or two species; those cited above are exceptions to the rule. If inappropriate worms do wind up in your dog or you, they'll soon be killed by the body's natural defense mechanisms. Nevertheless, human beings can develop a rare condition known as *larva migrans,* caused by immature worms that move through the skin or internal organs in their fruitless searching for appropriate host organs to live in and feed off. Until they find their biologically appropriate host, the worms will not live and mature. Each type of worm is parasitic to one particular animal. Rarely is there a crossover in hosts. Such parasites will die, but in the meantime can cause fever, dermatitis, and other reactions before finally succumbing to the immune system. The sure way to avoid *larva migrans* is to be sure your dogs are entirely worm-free. And do not allow them to kill rats and mice, whose intestines are almost always infected with parasites.

The one sure diagnosis for *all* types of worms is to have your dog's urine and feces examined by a competent veterinarian. Remember, however, that some worm species—hookworms, for instance—leave only sporadic traces in a dog's stool. So two or three different samples, collected on different days, must be analyzed before their presence can be ruled out. Once a dog has been wormed, a semiannual stool examination is considered prudent, because adult dogs can be reinfected by investigating feces containing roundworm eggs. But if a dog has had a more resilient parasite such as a tapeworm, or a number of bouts with roundworms (indicating a source of infection where the dog walks or plays), then it's better to have him checked every three months to be sure that worms don't get a foothold. This is especially important if your dog plays in areas where lots of other animals congregate. You don't need to take your pet in for an exam at these times unless he is experiencing other problems. Simply drop the fresh samples off at your vet. (Store the samples in a refrigerator if there is a delay in delivery.)

For a worm-infested dog, the nutrition problem is twofold: not only is his appetite decreased by the worms' presence but he also loses additional nourishment through the constant loss of blood, which in turn lowers his immune system's ability to fight these parasites. On the other hand, a dog who's well-nourished from the beginning seems to have less trouble keeping roundworms at bay. Studies done at England's National Institute for Medical Research indicate that puppies raised on a high-protein diet had smaller numbers of *toxicara canis* eggs in their feces than a control group of puppies fed merely adequate rations. In general, the high-protein puppies also suffered fewer of the side effects normally associated with worm infestations, such as diarrhea, emaciation, and discomfort.

In other words, one of the best preventive medicines against roundworms is an especially nourishing diet. And happily, there are a number of easy, practical ways to supplement your dog's ordinary meals, as we'll explain in the next chapter.

10

Supplementing Your Dog's Diet

 As recently as five years ago, many veterinarians and dog experts were saying that supplements weren't necessary as long as a dog was eating a balanced and nutritionally complete dog food. As one brochure put it, "Because reputable dog food manufacturers incorporate in their products all of the nutrients known to be needed by dogs, supplements are indicated only to tempt appetite or to correct a specific deficiency." Our own column in *Parents Magazine* stated that "vitamins are rarely needed with a proper diet regime, but on the other hand, they don't do any harm. Therefore, if it makes you feel better, add some."

Refined sugar, which is added to many processed foods for man and beast alike, can cause low blood sugar (hypoglycemia). It also interferes with the metabolism of calcium, iron, and potassium and it drastically lowers the body's resistance by hampering white blood cells' ability to ingest foreign particles and bacteria. Refined sugar has also been convincingly implicated in hyperactivity and aggressive behavior—so much so that in a recent murder trial, the defense attorney claimed his client wasn't responsible for his actions because junk food had warped his ability to tell right from wrong!

Basically, the "balanced" dog foods do contain all the nutrients your pet needs, and in the proper balance. It's likely that a smaller-sized dog can get all he needs from this commercial fare. But the problem is dog food manufacturers are not under the same restraints as the producers of human food. Pet foods can contain additives, flavor-enhancers, and carcinogens simply because it's not likely that any dog owner would sue the manufacturer—even if it could be proven that a pet died from eating a given chemical in a given brand. Now, as pet food becomes an even more profitable industry, more money is being poured into advertising and marketing gimmicks than into nutrition. No matter how good a given brand may be *today*, you have no guarantee that new processing techniques or additional additives won't erode its food value. If the FDA couldn't stop the manufacturers of flea collars from using cancer-causing chemicals, it's not going to regulate what other extras go into your pet's dog food.

Moreover, as we've explained in previous chapters, giving a dog what he's *known* to require may simply not be enough. The very fact that extra protein can help puppies throw off roundworm infestation has important implications. It's most likely that an extra measure of nutrients can help your pet over a wide range of other health and behavior problems—and there's increasing evidence that such is indeed the case.

A few years ago, a rumor spread among dog breeders

that extra doses of vitamin C could help prevent hip dysplasia in puppies. Pregnant dogs were fed one gram a day of sodium ascorbic crystals; puppies from three to six months received 500 mg a day, which was slowly increased until they too were getting a full gram of ascorbic acid a day. Of course, a dog can manufacture his own vitamin C, and the evidence that these supplements actually prevented instances of hip dysplasia was inconclusive. But there's no doubt that extra vitamin C has an effect on growth, at least in humans. In one study reported in the *Journal of the American Medical Association,* twins given 500 mg of vitamin C a day grew faster than their identical siblings who were given a placebo. In Denver, children who were deemed short for their age were found to have a zinc deficiency. Once they started taking zinc supplements, their growth accelerated again.

It seems logical that these findings should prove valid for dogs as well, especially since puppies and pregnant and nursing dogs are *known* to require extra nourishment. Ideally, of course, extra nutrients should start being administered well before the puppies' birth, thus ensuring that both parent dogs are in the best possible physical condition. Not surprisingly, females who were malnourished as puppies often grow up to have problems with reproduction, including difficult birthing caused by a poor formation of the pelvic bones. Iodine deficiency can result in sterility in females, and often in males as well. Obesity, too, is a rather effective means of canine birth control; fat males can become *permanently* sterile, and overweight females may fail to conceive.

EXTRA NUTRITION FOR BREEDING AND PREGNANCY

For dogs, between fifty-eight and sixty-eight days elapse between the time of mating and when the puppies are delivered. As soon as the female dog conceives, her nutritional needs jump by about 20 percent—and by her sixth week of pregnancy, she'll need at least 60 percent more food than she was eating before. It has already been established that newborn puppies have a higher survival rate if their mother is fed at least fifty milligrams of vitamin C during her pregnancy. Thus, it makes sense to begin increasing her diet and vitamin supplements *before* the mating, so that the new embryos have the benefit of the richest possible supply of nutrients when embedded in the wall of the uterus.

Strictly speaking, a pregnant dog is eating just about the same number of calories per pound of body weight as she was before—but as her developing litter takes on weight, her needs rise accordingly. Very small dogs may bear only one or two puppies, but this is still a major stress given the fact that smaller animals normally require more calories per pound of body weight. Similarly, large dogs who bear a large number of puppies may also consume much more—up to three times the volume of their earlier maintenance diet.

To help a pregnant dog digest the extra bulk, it helps to give her two meals a day, the first in the morning and the second at her regular mealtime. During her first month of pregnancy, an expectant mother should generally be fed the same high-calorie diet she was getting before she conceived except that more of those calories should be in the form of proteins and fewer in carbohydrates. Protein intake is bolstered during pregnancy because of its use in building tissue. (It can also help her combat any latent roundworm infection.) But do not feed a pregnant dog more than she needs. More meals put unnecessary fat reserves on both mother and the pups she is carrying. The strain on her system and overweight pups can make it significantly harder for her to give birth.

If a pregnant animal's diet is lacking in certain micronutrients for short periods, even days, congenital abnormalities can occur in the offspring. Lack of riboflavin can lead to skeletal deformities. The needs of a developing fetus vary widely from week to week, so any dietary shortfall can be far more serious if it comes during a crucial stage of development. The idea, therefore, is to make sure a pregnant dog has more than enough micronutrients throughout her gestation period.

Also important are moderately extra amounts of vitamin D (preferably in combination with a vegetable oil that ensures that this fat-soluble vitamin will be absorbed), calcium, or dolomite (a mineral compound with calcium and magnesium in equal amounts). All three micronutrients ensure that the offspring can develop without "withdrawing" supplies from their mother's body and thus weakening her. Just don't go the megadose route—that could be toxic. When it comes to micronutrients, it's vital that all minerals and vitamins be in proper proportions. Any imbalance can be damaging. An excess of vitamin A and the B-complex vitamins have been shown to cause congenital abnormalities, and too much D results in the calcification of certain organs. But extra doses of the nontoxic, water-soluble vitamins such as C are safe and can be given independently of any balanced supplement.

From the fourth week of pregnancy, the expectant mother's total intake should be gradually increased to match her naturally increasing weight. These rations should be maintained until she has stopped nursing and her litter is weaned. But after the sixth week of pregnancy, it may be wise to level off on her intake of carbohydrates and fats. During the last week of pregnancy, the unborn puppies will use extra calories to increase their growth inside the womb—if their mother is fed fattening foods, they will develop into overly large puppies and thus cause a difficult birth.

A pregnant dog should be walked at least once a day to help her maintain good muscle tone. It's a good idea, though, not to allow her any vigorous exercise, especially not during the last month of pregnancy. Of course, the dog will naturally slow her activity as she gains weight; but if she was provided with a good exercise program before conceiving, that should have a lasting benefit, ensuring that she'll still be in good shape when delivery occurs. As her pregnancy advances, you'll find that she needs to be taken out more and more often. The swelling uterus puts pressure on the bladder and large intestine, and she will need to relieve herself at shorter intervals.

LACTATION AND NURSING

After her puppies are born, keep her protein coming to stimulate extra milk secretion. Up to a third of the amino acids she ingests will go directly to her mammary glands. Generally, a nursing dog needs twice her normal protein; but if she's already being fed two to three times her basic rations, chances are her protein needs are already being met. Canine milk also contains very high quantities of fats and minerals, but this should be no problem if she's getting triple her normal amount of food.

Even though she is no longer carrying her puppies, you have to figure them as part of her body weight—inasmuch as she is providing 100 percent of their nourishment. It makes sense, then, to weigh the litter soon after birth and weekly thereafter; their increasing poundage will make sense of the apparently staggering amount of food their mother is consuming.

Also make sure she's getting extra calcium, since a great deal of it will be secreted in her milk. A severe calcium deficiency results in a serious condition called eclampsia. After about two weeks of nursing have depleted her body's calcium reserves, a mother dog may become lethargic and begin shivering, a result of lower-than-normal body temperature. Meanwhile, her heartbeat will become irregular and weaken, and a continued calcium drain through nursing will lead to convulsions and death. Remember, though, that calcium must be given in balance with phosphorus for a dog to absorb it properly; the correct ratio is six parts calcium to five of phosphorus. Milk has the proper ratio, but cow's milk can cause diarrhea in a dog. *Powdered* milk or bone meal added to her normal food should not present any digestive problems. Canned dog food will usually say on the label if it has been fortified with calcium; if not, a bone meal supplement is definitely in order. In any case, keep giving the mother the same nutrient supplements she was getting during pregnancy. Her food and micronutrient intake should stay high until her litter is about a month old and weaning has begun.

SUPPLEMENTS FOR GROWING PUPPIES

Once weaning begins, you must start cutting back rapidly on the mother's food. As she eats less and less, the puppies will be eating more and more on their own. If they are separated from her during the day but allowed to nurse at night, that will help them adjust more quickly to solid food while still preventing congestion of her teats. During weaning you can introduce them to the same balanced vitamin-and-mineral supplement you were giving their mother.

Many micronutrients are compromised or destroyed in the cooking process that's necessary to make carbohydrates digestible. The virtue of vitamin supplements is that you can add them at the last minute, right before your dog eats, and thus be assured he's receiving their full benefit. Better yet, the nutrients in any supplement are balanced for ideal absorption, and you can thus be sure exactly how much of each one your dog is getting. Supplements for dogs come in liquid and pill form, but the powdered ones are by far the most convenient; you just sprinkle them on the food—you don't have to otherwise disguise them or feed them separately. In selecting a supplement, look for one in which the minerals are *chelated;* in this form they are easier for the body to absorb and can help the kidneys dispose of potentially toxic wastes.

FEEDING YOUR DOG A PILL OR LIQUID
MEDICATION/VITAMIN

Sooner or later, there will come a time when you have to give your dog a vitamin pill or some special medication that your veterinarian has prescribed. Open your dog's mouth and push the pill far back in his mouth, almost in the throat. Close your dog's mouth and hold it closed. Tilt his head back and slowly rub his throat, stroking downward. When he sticks his tongue out, he has swallowed the pill. If you can't get your dog to take a pill this way, you can try sneaking the pill into the center of a cheese wedge or ball of hamburger. But never mix a large pill or capsule with food, because the size will be prohibitive to your dog who normally wolfs down food.

To administer liquid vitamins and minerals, use a plastic eyedropper or a special dosage syringe, which you can get from a vet, that draws up the required amount. Then, holding the dog's mouth shut, insert the nozzle or eyedropper inside the loose flesh of his muzzle behind his canine teeth. Lift his head up, and squeeze slowly and gently. He'll swallow it.

Many of the medications your veterinarian will prescribe for your dog are the same types of substances used to treat people with similar problems. Of course, the dosages are much smaller, relative to the patient's body weight. That's why you must not dose your dog with human medications: it's not the content, but the overdose, that usually causes the problem. Sedatives, diet pills, and other depressant drugs that have serious side effects on people are only worse when given to a dog. However, you can safely administer an antacid to control vomiting and a binding antidiarrhea agent to stop your dog's diarrhea, as long as you scale down the dose.

Also remember that if your dog is taking prescription antibiotics, they can wipe out some of the bacteria in his large intestine, which can result in more diarrhea. Feed him a little yogurt, which contains the same basic strain of bacteria, to help "stock the pool" again.

PROTEIN DEFICIENCY AND ITS CONSEQUENCES

Coprophagy of Cat Droppings

One woman followed our program with her first dog, with great success. Then she bought herself two cats. But when she added a second puppy to the household, he soon started chewing on the draperies and furniture, urinating and defecating indoors, and putting on weight—acting exactly as if he had been eating the wrong food in wrong amounts. But since his owner had been following our directions to the letter, we looked for some other logical reason for the puppy's misbehavior. Was the dog getting food elsewhere? The woman assured us that no one else could be feeding him. Was he getting into the older dog's food—or that of the cats? No, she made sure every animal ate separately at a different time. Was she using some household cleanser to which the dog might be allergic? Had there been *any* changes in the normal household routine?

After some thought, the woman admitted there was a

new development with her cats: shortly after she had brought the new puppy home, they'd stopped using the litter box. She reasoned that the cats—who, she claimed, were naturally clean, private, and aloof—must have found a more private spot outside. Exactly where they were going to relieve themselves she didn't know but she hadn't found any cat droppings in the house. We suggested that her new puppy might be accountable for the disappearance of the droppings. The woman was appalled. "Impossible," she insisted. "No dog of mine would do such a disgusting thing." The next day, however, she called to apologize. After we left, the puppy had crawled up on her bed and thrown up all over her new down quilt, thereby proving our conjecture. On our advice, the woman bought a new enclosed litter box, and within a couple of weeks the new dog was shaping up nicely.

It's unfortunately true that dogs find the droppings of cats—and of horses, and several other animals—irresistible. City dogs walked in a cow pasture will often pause to munch on cowflops. Most authorities agree that this disgusting habit is a throwback to a dog's scavenger ancestry, when he had to search for extra nutrients, whether B vitamins formed by intestinal bacteria or vegetable fiber broken down and softened by another beast's digestion. In cat droppings, though, the main attraction is probably protein. Cats demand a diet that's far richer in protein than what is right for a dog, and their feces are full of undigested amino acids that a dog can smell quite easily.

Coprophagy of Own Feces

As some hapless owners have discovered, a dog will sometimes eat his *own* feces as well. Pets often pick up this wretched trait after being confined in a boarding kennel with other dogs, where the cages are not regularly cleaned. The theory goes that when a number of dogs are fed *en masse,* the lower-ranking members of this pack may not be getting their full share. And if another dog hasn't digested his food thoroughly (not unlikely, in the case of an anxious fearful animal who's suddenly deprived of familiar surroundings and confined with other strange dogs), a hungry dog's nose may tell him that these feces are still fair game.

A dog can also develop this habit on his own. Chances are such an offender isn't digesting his *own* food properly, perhaps because it contains certain nutrients he can't absorb. Also, a well-trained dog who has misbehaved indoors will sometimes try to consume the "evidence" in order to avoid punishment. There are a number of logical remedies, all of which you should try at the same time.

First, walk your dog frequently and dispose of his feces promptly so that he can't return to them. If he does, watch him and reprimand him harshly, as you would for any other garbage scavenging (see Chapter 7). Also, switch the brand of food he's eating—the new blend may well prove more digestible. At the same time, you can feed your dog a substance that will make his feces totally unpalatable. Vets most commonly recommend glutamine hydrochloride, also known as glutamic acid. Health food stores carry it as a food supplement; and pet stores also sell it under various brand names. For a medium-sized dog of forty pounds, the recommended dosage is 100 mg, two to three times daily.

You can also dust his food with meat tenderizer. Look for the salt-free variety with natural ingredients. (Most meat tenderizers contain a great deal of sodium, which in large quantities is not good for any mammal.) Just before you serve your dog's meal, sprinkle on the tenderizer, using just a bit more than the directions on the package suggest. These substances work by breaking down proteins; thus, in effect, you are predigesting your dog's meal for him. Ideally, his stomach will be able to finish the job so that his feces will then contain too few amino acids to be tempting. If you can't find a salt-free meat tenderizer, papaya enzyme will do almost as well.

It's important to add these substances just before your dog begins eating; otherwise, the proteins may entirely disintegrate before he has a chance to consume them. But the all-around best way to forestall feces eating in the first place is to make sure that your dog's diet has plenty of easily digestible protein from the very start.

ESTIMATING YOUR PET'S PROTEIN NEED

One can of dog food usually contains no more than twenty-five grams of *usable* protein—that is, protein that the dog can digest and absorb effectively. But an adult dog weighing twenty pounds may require up to thirty-four grams of usable protein a day; and puppies and pregnant and nursing mothers need about sixty-five grams daily.

To judge the exact amount of protein in any dog food, check the label. The manufacturer has usually made these calculations for you, but they are only *estimates*. No matter how well mixed the food is, the actual nutrient levels can vary by up to 10 percent. Also, when estimating your dog's protein intake, remember that *all* moist dog foods contain water. Thus 120 grams of meat does not automatically represent 120 grams of protein; after the weight of the water and fats are subtracted, the actual weight of protein may be thirty grams or less.

If your commercial dog food comes up short, the answer is *not* to feed your dog extra beef. In terms of a dog's nutritional needs, twelve and a half ounces of raw beef may contain the right number of calories but will provide too much fat plus not enough iron, cobalt, copper, iodine, magnesium, phosphorus, or potassium. Beef is also short on vitamins A, D, and E, and the ratio of calcium to phosphorus is wrong. In any case, many veterinarians advise that regular meat be no more than 40 percent of a dog's daily meal, simply because lean muscle tissue lacks many of the unbankable micronutrients your dog needs. Beef, pork, and other red meats also create more nitrogenous wastes when metabolized, which puts the kidneys under additional strain to cleanse these by-products from the bloodstream.

By contrast, beans, chicken, cooked eggs, fish, rice, tofu, and other vegetable proteins are "cleaner burning" and don't force your dog to drink more water. They also provide fiber, and, happily, the heat of cooking causes some vegetables to increase their percentage of fiber as the water boils away. (What you want to avoid, of course, is overcooking; the whole idea is to keep as many micronutrients intact as possible, for your dog and for you.)

Another way to boost your pet's protein intake is to feed him foods that interact with one another to make their proteins more digestible. Individually, one and a half cups of brown rice and a half a cup of beans contain some twenty grams of usable protein. But when eaten together, their usable protein total rises to twenty-nine grams. Milk can unlock extra protein from rolled oats, from combinations of cornmeal and tofu, and also from eggs, brewer's yeast, and oats. But because most dogs have trouble digesting raw milk, you should substitute a third of a cup of powdered milk or a half of a cup of cottage cheese, either of which has the same protein content as one cup of whole milk.

If only 40 percent of your dog's diet is meat, then the rest of the bulk (and protein) *must* come from vegetables and grains. So you can supplement your dog's diet with organ meats from the butcher, such as kidney and raw liver, as long as you mix them with appropriate quantities of cooked rice and beans. Chop the meat and simmer it for about ten minutes before mixing it with the vegetables.

Remember that how protein is stored and prepared has a direct effect on its quality. Moisture content, length of cooking time, and the presence of fats and sugars can all affect its biological value. For example, heat can bind certain sugars to amino acids in such a way that the body cannot use them. This is why boiled milk contains incomplete proteins but pasteurized milk (which is treated at a lower temperature) suffers no protein damage.

You can also give your dog a cooked egg or two. But never feed your dog raw eggs, regardless of what a veterinarian may recommend; raw egg whites deactivate the body's biotin and weaken the bones. And keep in mind that eggs are high in cholesterol.

Dr. David Kornfeld, professor of Nutrition at the University of Pennsylvania's Veterinary School, suggests a homemade protein-rich "side dish" that can be fed to dogs along with or in place of their everyday commercial dog food (coprophagy and other indications of protein deficiency may require this type of rich supplementation).

- Mix ⅔ cup of brown rice with ⅓ cup bone-free, cooked, ground "organ" meat—glands, heart, liver, lungs, tongue, tripe, and so forth. Add to this basic cooked mixture a supplement of 3 tablespoons of bone meal, 1 ounce of ground liver, ¼ of a teaspoon of iodized salt, and 1 teaspoon of corn oil. Serve fresh, feeding 1 cup per twenty-eight pounds of your dog's body weight every day, and shape the rest into patties and freeze for future use.

Even if you don't go to the trouble of cooking special meals for your dog, we do think it is advisable to sprinkle his daily food with wheat germ—especially for puppies and pregnant females.

CHEWING "SUPPLEMENTS"

Even a dog who's being fed a proper diet still enjoys chewing. He simply won't be *compelled* to chew and is more likely to obey your directions as to what objects he's not supposed to touch. Of course it's easier for him to obey if he has something he *may* gnaw on should he get restless or bored. The problem is, a dog's jaws exert so much pressure that any chew-toy is a sometime thing. Common sense demands that you rule out anything fragile that can be easily ripped, torn, splintered, or swallowed. That rules out latex toys, anything with a squeaker or a bell inside, chicken bones, tennis balls, anything wooden or plastic, and discarded clothing—puppies have been known to gulp down whole socks!

The very best chew-toy is a very hard rubber ball, a nylon bone, or a *natural* rawhide chew-"bone," available at most pet shops. Look carefully at the color. Natural rawhide is yellowish in color; and if the rawhide is white or oystershell, it has been bleached chemically and is probably still impregnated with some of those chemicals. The whole idea is to give your dog something that resists his jaws as much as possible while still providing *some* give. And though rawhide and rubber are supposed to be heavy-duty items, keep an eye on them. When they begin to look tattered and definitely the worse for wear, replace them. When they finally start to crumble, they do so all at once, and your dog will be able to swallow chunks of them when your back is turned.

As you know, dogs make fast associations. Therefore, if you give a puppy only one or two toys, and regularly replace them with nearly identical ones that smell and taste alike, it'll be far easier for him to sort out what's chewable and what you've forbidden him to touch. (This is another argument against letting a dog chew on old clothing or footwear; this teaches him that it's fine to chew on *any* clothing or footwear.)

It's best not to give your dog any bones at all because the grease and residual aromas tend to rub off on rugs, furniture, and other household objects. Then, following his nose, your dog will assume it's okay to chew on them too. Besides, bones can be dangerous. They can splinter and puncture the esophagus, or semi-isolid bone fragments can become impacted in the large intestine, causing a total blockage that your veterinarian will have to fix—if your dog doesn't die first. If you insist on giving your dog a bone, the best type to ask your butcher to give you is the center part of a big beef shank bone with the knuckles on each end sawed off. This will last a good while without splintering. Unless you can let your dog chew on meat bones outside the house, make the bone relatively sanitary by boiling it, although this takes away a good deal of the pleasure from the canine point of view.

FAT AND "FLAVOR" SUPPLEMENTS

Any vitamin supplement you're giving your dog must contain fatty acids, expensive and perishable though they may be. Since dogs love the smell of oil, fats are a flavor-enhancer and can be spread or lightly sprinkled on food to make it more palatable—and used as a temporary bribe to ease a dog over dietary switches. If your pet is on a dry food regimen, he's probably not getting nearly enough polyunsaturated fats. So give him one teaspoon of vegetable oil daily for every thirty pounds of his body weight.

For finicky eaters or dogs who have lost their appetites because of sickness or injury, there's a variation of the last method we outlined in Chapter 4: simply add those cherished food scraps to your dog's regular fare. Just be sure the scraps don't contain excess fat, spices, and small bones. The only danger is that your dog will get so addicted to these morsels that he'll hold out for larger amounts. If you must add them as flavor-enhancers, think of them as chocolate chips, sprinkled here and there to provide hints of flavor, but not as a main ingredient.

If your dog is already enjoying the after-dinner "one taste" ritual, then he's probably getting all the table scraps he really needs. If you are thrifty enough to want to add leftovers to your dog's main meal, make them *kitchen* scraps—minced chicken giblets, diced (and lightly simmered) vegetable parings, a teaspoon of cooking oil, any leftover rice, plus the water in which vegetables have been cooked. These don't make a dog into a flavor junkie and do give him certain nutritional value.

11
Dietary Troubleshooting

Around 400 B.C., the Greek physician Hippocrates used to tell his students, "Let your food be your medicine, and your medicine be your food." This chapter isn't intended as a substitute for a consultation with your veterinarian, or as a guide to what symptoms may signify. (To give just one example, a swollen belly can indicate a number of ailments from hormone imbalance to liver trouble and malnutrition, and it's best to let a vet make the diagnosis.) Rather, what follows is a concise alphabetical listing of a number of canine complaints—and what you can do about them at home, simply through diet before and after taking the dog to the vet. Since each of the following problems is at least partly diet-related, it's largely up to you how quickly your pet gets over them.

APPETITE LOSS

A dog may easily skip a meal or eat half-heartedly, especially in summer when the heat is getting to him and he doesn't need as many calories anyway. That's nothing to worry about. But a dog who's been ill with an infection or who is recovering from an injury or surgical operation (such as spaying) may have little appetite. Since the convalescent dog needs even *more* nutrition than normal, this can be dangerous.

Dogs are often reluctant to eat where they sleep; if possible, coax your dog over to where his feeding bowl is usually kept. The sight, smells, and associations should help get his digestion going. Try lacing the food with some of his favorite flavor supplements—beef broth, avocado, poultry (chicken is bland and easily digestible), and lightly cooked kidney or liver are all possible bribes.

Part of the problem may be that the animal is simply feeling poorly. He may respond better if you sit down on the floor beside him, pat him gently, scratch him behind the ears, talk to him and praise him, then offer a little food in his bowl. If he licks at it, praise him lavishly. When he finishes that, give him another small dose. (Small portions will make him more eager to finish what he has.) If the dog is very weak, you can offer—or spoon-feed him—chicken soup. Dip your finger in it if he's reluctant and rub a taste on your dog's gums to let him know what he's missing. The slightly fatty residue should tempt your dog's sense of smell. Be sure to let any such broth cool to room temperature.

If he spits out the food and absolutely refuses to eat,

take him to the vet. A weakened dog who's totally indifferent to nourishment may need vitamin injections or intravenous feeding to build up his strength.

BAD BREATH

Bad breath is a frequent complaint among dog owners—and a frustrating one, because there can be so many different causes. Your dog may have just chomped on some smelly tidbit; then again, he may have gum disease or even kidney problems. (A dog with weak kidneys will have an abnormally high level of urea in his blood, making his breath smell of urine.) But by far the most common cause of bad breath in dogs is tooth decay, or simply dirty teeth that have built up a layer of plaque and tartar.

A puppy starts out with twenty-eight baby or milk teeth, which are replaced with forty-two permanent teeth by the time he's about six months old. Unlike your teeth, your dog's are spaced widely enough apart so that they don't trap food in between them. That has led to a rumor that a dog's mouth is somehow cleaner than a human's and that dogs, therefore, don't require preventive dental care. Actually, *any* apparently "clean" body surface (including the skin) supports a hefty population of resident bacteria. And your dog is constantly introducing new strains of microorganisms into his mouth when he uses his teeth and tongue to investigate street objects. Even more bacteria will thrive in the plaque—basically, solidified minerals from his saliva—that builds up around the base of his teeth just below the gum line.

Cleaning Teeth

Biscuits may help clean your dog's molars but will hardly help keep his whole mouth spick-and-span. Nor will a rawhide chew-toy get into all the cracks. Water picks, designed to blast food particles from between human molars, will make your dog choke; toothpaste is too highly flavored and will make him spit and cough. Just moisten an old toothbrush with water or, at most, some baking soda, and give your dog's teeth a weekly scrubbing.

To brush effectively, hold his muzzle closed and work the brush gently back and forth, just inside the jowls. This should not only freshen his breath but also forestall the conditions that lead to tooth decay and gum disease, both of which have to be treated by a vet. Your dog may not like the tickling on his gums and may at first try to pull away. You have to be insistent and make him stay. If you feed him a treat after the cleaning (not as a reward but to condition him to accept the experience), he's more likely to sit still the next time you approach with the toothbrush. Finally, let him drink some water to rinse his mouth, or swab his mouth with a damp washrag to get rid of any lingering debris.

Some breeds are more prone to dental trouble than others. Boston terriers, bulldogs, Pekinese, and pugs, for example, have been deliberately bred to have short, pushed-in muzzles; these dogs' jawbones don't always have room for all forty-two permanent teeth. Tooth crowding is also a problem with Chihuahuas and miniature poodles, whose sharp milk teeth do not always fall out. So when the adult teeth erupt, they often come up *beside* the baby teeth. The dog has two sets of intermingled teeth and may look somewhat like the poster for *Jaws*. Have the baby teeth pulled or food will start to be trapped in between them.

If your dog is high-strung and nervous, or if he gulps his food, his frequent burps may be confused with bad breath. Try adding a very small amount of chopped parsley to his meal. If the "bad breath" is basically malodorous burps from poor digestion, then he should also be suffering from flatulence. (See Flatulence, page 230.) Charcoal pills and a change in diet should help.

BLOAT: GASTRIC TORSION

Bloat occurs when the contents of the stomach ferment, releasing gases that cause the stomach to swell. As the stomach continues to expand, pressure is put on all the vital organs. Eventually the stomach enlarges to the point where the pressure on the vital organs becomes life threatening. (For example, breathing becomes difficult because of constriction of the lungs.) Ultimately, the stomach gradually rips itself apart causing internal hemorrhaging. Death follows either from the loss of blood or from destruction of one of the vital organs by pressure exerted by the distended stomach.

Normally a dog's digestion in the stomach is much too rapid and food passes through too quickly to allow this type of gaseous fermentation. But certain conditions can combine to cause this problem in a dog. First of all, it happens most often with larger dogs, occurring in dogs who have just eaten a heavy meal, then drunk a quantity of water, and been let outside to romp around. The weight of the food causes the stomach to swing back and forth. If enough of momentum develops, the dog's stomach flips over, sealing itself off at both ends, thus preventing the release of food. Sometimes the stomach doesn't even have to flip; its weight can simply make it drop so low that the tubes leading into and out of the stomach become so constricted they actually close off. In addition, simply eating very dry food and drinking excessive water can cause the food to expand rapidly. Excessive gases are thereby released more quickly than the stomach can tolerate and it churns violently trying to bring the food under control. The uncontrolled movement makes the stomach contort in such a way that it becomes stopped up. Activity on your dog's part is therefore not necessarily needed to cause gastric torsion.

An afflicted dog will look and probably feel as though he has a basketball in his stomach. He will stiffen in pain and walk in tight circles, instinctively trying to make himself vomit. If he does, he will usually regurgitate foam. Too often, owners mistake this frenzied "dance" for simple neurotic behavior and reprimand the dog or send him out of the room—which can amount to a death sentence. As the stomach distends, it seals itself even more tightly, leading to death. You should get your dog to a veterinarian for treatment as soon as possible.

Our weimaraner Plum suffered bloat several times. The first instance was when we left him with friends and he got into a garbage can and ate his fill. Fortunately, our friends got him to the vet in time. But for some reason, he became prone to gastric torsion attacks, even when he hadn't overeaten or had had too much exercise.

Fortunately, we learned the signs of bloat and were able to recognize an attack within minutes. Several times we were able to save him by passing a special tube down his esophagus that allowed stomach gas to escape, a procedure that most veterinarians can show you how to perform. One time we were in the car, with no tube handy, when we saw Plum begin to expand around the middle. But as luck would have it, we happened to be jolting along a very bumpy road, which shook his stomach loose.

Obviously, prevention is the better medicine. Teach your dog never to eat garbage, and be sure his food is crushed up finely enough so that he's forced to eat slowly. If he's a committed gobbler, you may want to try feeding him his meal in two or three installments over the course of fifteen minutes or so. Definitely presoak any dry food, because if it's puffed or otherwise expanded, it has excess volume. For a bloat-prone dog, the after-dinner walk is still okay, but withhold any vigorous exercise until you're positive that digestion is complete and most of his meal has entered the small intestine. We have covered this same advice earlier, but are repeating it here for emphasis because it can be a matter of life and death.

THE CONVALESCENT DOG

Whatever the reason for his being there, having to spend the night at the vet's is stressful for your pet. Any dog will usually be overjoyed to be home again and will probably expend a lot of energy in proving the point to you, unless he's very weak or ill or in pain. In any case, your canine patient needs extra doses of nourishment to speed his healing and get him back to his old, healthy self.

When it comes to healing, vitamin C is getting to be an almost knee-jerk reaction among nutritionists. In humans, it's been hailed as a possible way to cut down on the incidence of everything from the common cold to herpes—simply because it helps boost the effectiveness of the immune system. Vitamin C has also been targeted as a stress-fighting vitamin that helps the adrenal glands and other components of the body's fight-or-flight mechanism. Your dog, of course, manufactures his own ascorbic acid, but extra doses have been proven to hasten the healing of wounds. We've already outlined in Chapter 10 the benefits that extra vitamin C can have for young puppies. It makes sense, then, to give your back-at-home pet at least 500 mg of ascorbic acid daily, plus all the water he wants. (Since vitamin C is water-soluble, his system will automatically flush away what it doesn't use.) Your dog will also need plenty of protein supplements to help rebuild any tissues and speed healing; in addition, extra protein has been shown to help dogs synthesize the antibodies they need to fight bacterial and viral infections.

It's a safe bet that whatever food he was given at the vet's won't match what you were feeding him at home. Therefore—especially if he's being switched to a prescription diet—you can expect a bit of digestive upset, possibly diarrhea, which can also be a symptom of earlier shock or general nervousness.

A dog will often perceive a stay at the vet's as punishment, thinking you've abandoned him and had him locked up for some misdeed he can't remember. And so he may be submissive, sheepish, even cowed upon his return home. Give him plenty of attention and affection to prove to him he's a good dog. This, too, might be a great time to introduce any sudden changes of diet or routine that you've been planning, such as a switch to a therapeutic prescription diet. Your dog will be in a far more receptive mood his first day home and less likely to pit his will against yours.

It's perfectly all right to welcome him with a very light meal in the morning for the first couple of days. This gives him just a touch of extra nourishment and stimulates his digestive tract, which may be out of sync. If he needs to be walked more often, do that too; a recuperating dog will bounce back faster if he doesn't lie on his mat all day. The outdoor walk is a gentle, thoroughly beneficial kind of exercise.

If your dog is recuperating from surgery, add some vitamin E to his food, together with poultry fat or vegetable oil. Vitamin E is reputed to help prevent scarring, and the extra fat will ensure that more of it is carried into your dog's bloodstream and on its way to halt inflammation and speed healing. In humans, vitamin E has been associated with the spontaneous disappearance of warts and other benign growths on the skin, so this might be a possible supplement for any dog who suffers from moles or growths on the face or eyelids (a fairly frequent occurrence in older dogs).

If any specific medicines or antibiotics have been prescribed, check with your vet before giving your dog any extras. Certain minerals can inhibit the effectiveness of medicines: zinc, for example, hampers the effectiveness of tetracycline, and penicillin is compromised when taken with acidic fruit juices. This means you may want to let your dog drink water to dilute his stomach acids before you give him an antibiotic pill.

DIABETES

Diabetes is a condition that demands close supervision by a veterinarian who will probably want to keep the dog for a few days for testing so that the animal's correct insulin and food balance can be determined. Thereafter at home, you must keep a close check on the dog's diet, regulate and inject the amount of insulin he needs, and time his exercise to coincide with proper levels of blood sugar. Your vet can supply you with a special tape, similar to litmus paper, for testing your dog's urine to be sure that his blood sugar (or, more accurately, the quantity of sugar being eliminated through the kidneys) is within bounds. A single injection of insulin every morning seems adequate for most pets, but to keep the blood sugar from peaking the diabetic dog often needs more than one meal a day.

If dogs develop diabetes early in life, it makes sense to have them spayed or castrated. First, a neutered dog is more docile, more easy-going, and less prone to sudden spurts of activity that can upset his blood sugar level. And, in the long run, it's better that dogs with genetic defects not be allowed to pass their problems along to succeeding generations.

DULL COAT OR FUR

This is a common symptom of malnutrition, except in the case of a pregnant or nursing dog whose coat should return to its previous luster not long after her puppies are weaned. Even so, you might want to add fatty acids (present in butter, chicken fat, and the better vitamin supplements) to give her coat back its shine. If the supplements you're using don't *specify* fatty acids in their contents, get another brand that does. Fatty acids are usually in short supply in the semimoist and dry foods, largely because they're expensive and do not have as long a shelf life as the other ingredients.

FLATULENCE

Every dog will pass some gas once in a while, and this is no cause for concern. On the other hand, a pet who's constantly polluting the atmosphere needs dietary investigation. If your vet rules out worms, other possible causes include old age, nervousness, improper feeding, recent sickness, or colic—all of which result in incomplete digestion.

Try changing your dog's food, for starters. Often a pet will develop an allergy to some ingredient in commercial dog food and, when fed an allergy-free prescription diet, his health improves dramatically and flatulence disappears. Especially in older dogs, whose digestive tracts are notoriously more sluggish, insufficiently cooked grains and cereals are the worst offenders; but also make sure your dog isn't getting too much protein or carbohydrate for his age, weight, and activity level.

One supplemental remedy for gas is charcoal pills, available from a pharmacist or a veterinarian. Adjust the recommended dosage according to your dog's body weight. Also, try increasing his ration of *well*-cooked vegetables; a high-fiber diet should help move food through the large intestine before it has a chance to ferment.

As a last resort, keep watch on your dog when he's eating. An animal who bolts his food is not only consuming chunks that are harder to digest but he's also swallowing air—especially if his dry food hasn't been presoaked long enough. (Up to 70 percent of the gas in the digestive tract is thought to be swallowed air.) Mash the food down and add a bit more water so that all air bubbles float to the surface. Then make sure your dog gets more walks and light exercise, not only to stimulate digestion but also to let him pass gas while he's safely outside.

Meanwhile, if you find the smell annoying or embarrassing, light a match, hold it up in the air and let it burn for a few seconds, then snuff it out. The smell of sulphur will mask and help dissipate the offending aroma.

FRACTURES

A broken bone needs extra calcium (and, of course, phosphorus) in order to heal quickly and soundly. It's better to administer an all-around vitamin supplement so you won't risk any imbalances that might damage your dog's health. Too, this way insures that he's getting plenty of iron (to help build red blood cells) and other trace elements needed for the growth of healthy bones.

GASTROINTESTINAL PROBLEMS

Certain diseases and conditions predispose a dog to chronic vomiting and diarrhea. Treatment must be handled by a vet. At home, however, you have a double problem when it comes to feeding: the animal isn't absorbing enough nutrients because of the uproar in his digestive tract, and too rich a diet may upset his system further. Your most important responsibility then, is to make sure your dog gets no table scraps or other unauthorized supplements and isn't allowed to taste or even sniff garbage while outside. (At this point, the last thing he needs is a worm infection.)

In general, the veterinarian will probably suggest a bland diet with little or no vegetable fiber. Make sure the dog is getting plenty of water-soluble vitamins, because a dehydrated or malnourished dog will usually have depleted his reserve of B vitamins. Give protein in very digestible form: cooked eggs, cottage cheese, and glandular "organ meat" with little or no animal fats. (Vegetable oils are more easily digestible.) Also, be sure any cooked foods have a chance to cool down to room temperature.

A dog who has been vomiting may be dehydrated: let him lap water frequently, but only a little at a time. If he seems to be losing more fluid than he's taking in, your vet may want to give him special solutions of electrolytes, perhaps intravenously.

LICK GRANULOMA (HOT SPOTS)

As we've already explained in the Introduction, this whole syndrome is usually associated with the wrong diet. Yet an amazing number of people in the dog world seem to accept lick granuloma as a matter of course. After we prescribed a canned-food diet for the chow chow (see the Introduction), the dog's sores cleared up promptly. Yet the breeder from whom the owner had bought Natasha said, "This breed of dog always has sores, especially in summer. As a matter of fact, most dogs get sores like that in the summer. You just treat them with cortisone, and they'll go away."

All lick granulomas should be treated with a diet change, *not* with cortisone as some veterinarians recommend. Too much cortisone can have bad side effects. Our point of view is that it's cheaper (and certainly can do no harm) to simply change the dog's diet *first*, before embarking on a regimen of costly and possibly ineffective drugs. Then, if the dog keeps on licking and scratching at himself, take him to the vet. The problem will sometimes turn out to be a near-invisible scratch or cut between the toes (especially if he's licking the pad of one foot). Roughened or balding skin can be a symptom of mites or chiggers, which burrow into the skin, ringworm (a fungus infection), or a number of ailments conveniently lumped under the collective title of "contact dermatitis"—or, in lay language, skin allergy. The problem with such rashes is that they're self-perpetuating: they itch, so the dog scratches; this irritates the skin even more and opens it to more allergens; this causes more itching, so the dog scratches. . . .

Punishing the dog when you see him licking or scratching will only add to his misery, since it's impossible for you to reprimand him constantly and consistently. He's certain to gnaw and dig at himself at night, or when you aren't around. He should be checked for fleas or ticks. Occasionally, too, longer-haired dogs will accumulate burrs or devil's pitchforks in their hair—or the hair itself may bunch up and mat under the friction of the dog's walking. We once saw a border collie with what appeared to be a large flat tumor on the inside of her leg. It was just a highly compacted ball of fur that needed nothing more than quick "surgery" with a sharp pair of scissors.

Certain ointments, available from your veterinarian, have a numbing or anesthetic effect. But you must be prepared to apply them frequently to keep their soothing effect from wearing off. A suitably vile-tasting ointment will often deter your dog from licking, but some dogs will keep on regardless, simply because the itch is worse than the bad taste—or they will start scratching instead. If this is the case, bandaging the "hot spot" or fitting the dog with a cone-shaped Elizabethan collar or other restraint so that he can't reach the sore spot may allow it to heal unmolested.

LIVER TROUBLE

This is a job for your vet to handle. Any liver insufficiency means that your dog will have trouble metabolizing the nutrients he absorbs from his food—particularly fats and proteins. This, in turn, calls for changes in diet, as well as medication to prompt the liver to do whatever it's not doing.

Prevention is the best policy. A dog's liver can more or less repair and take care of itself, unless it's damaged by poisonous substances, which isn't likely unless your animal gets into tainted garbage. Since its major function is to detoxify incoming nutrients, the liver is literally the body's first line of defense against poisons. Therefore, most toxins your dog consumes will hit his liver first—and hardest. (See Poisonings.)

MALNUTRITION

Malnutrition is hardly likely for your pet if you've been following the guidelines throughout this book. But you may have a dog who was abandoned and suffered near-starvation before you got him. And once in a while, some hormone or glandular condition will affect an animal's absorption of nutrients. In any case, here are warning signs to watch for.

- *Evidence of early (or before birth) malnutrition:* Poor growth; bone deformity; irregular alignment of permanent teeth; lethargic behavior; difficulty in conceiving or in bearing healthy puppies
- *Evidence of short-term malnutrition:* Dry, dull coat; poor resistance to diseases; slow healing of cuts; slow growth; poor appetite; low energy
- *Evidence of long-term malnutrition:* Red, dull eyes; emaciation; dull coat; slow blood-clotting time; lethargy; bald patches; skin, tongue, and mouth ulcers; general weakness; muscle spasms; frequent colds and infections

As one brochure has put it, a malnourished pet looks bad, feels bad, and performs badly. Good nourishment not only improves your dog's looks but also boosts his immune system so that he can easily fight off the bacterial infections and other problems to which a malnourished dog might otherwise succumb.

PANCREATIC PROBLEMS

Pancreas Insufficiency

Pancreas insufficiency means that the dog's small intestine doesn't receive enough enzymes for proper digestion, and food is passed in more or less its original state. The dog will have large, bulky, smelly feces that often have an odor of rancid fat, since a good deal of the fats the dog is eating aren't emulsified but simply passed on into the colon.

At the same time, the dog will begin to show signs of malnutrition: loss of weight, a thin, dull coat, and a ravenous appetite. He must be fed a diet that's very digestible to start with—in other words, with high biological value. On top of that, your veterinarian can supply you with pancreatic enzymes in powder form. About two hours before feeding your dog, sprinkle his food with the powder and leave it in a warm, moist spot—essentially, this lets the food be digested while it's still in his bowl. Then, just before serving, add to the food some bile salts. It's also a good idea to treat a pancreas-weakened dog like a puppy, giving him two small meals a day rather than one large one that may be more difficult for his digestive tract to handle. Once the problem is under control, your dog's appetite should decrease along with the volume of his stool, and signs of malnutrition should vanish not long after.

Pancreatitis

Pancreatitis is just the opposite of pancreatic insufficiency; here, the gland is overstimulated, producing more enzymes than are necessary. Some veterinarians advise giving a dog a diet that's *deliberately* harder to digest than the average to help soak up some of those extra enzymes. Pancreatitis (which tends to flare up now and again) can be controlled by regulating the dog's diet—something we have already recommended for all dogs. Eliminate rich foods, especially fatty ones or those with excessive sweeteners that can trigger an attack. Semimoist food, which we never recommend under any circumstances, with its high content of corn syrup is especially irritating to the pancreas.

Keep a dog who has pancreatic flare-ups on a bland, low-fat, low-sugar diet. This is not a substitute for veterinary therapy which is a must for this condition. The pancreas provides the body's most important food digesting enzymes. As such it needs expert and constant monitoring.

PERINEAL OR RECTAL DISEASE

Here the problem is basically one of location. If a dog is recuperating from spaying, or if the anal glands have abscessed, the animal may find it too painful to defecate. The answer is to feed a low-residue, low-fiber diet until healing is complete. Even though an all-meat diet can cause malnutrition over a long period, fresh meat produces very little residue and it's worth trying for a few days, as long as you add a vitamin and mineral supplement. Cottage cheese, cooked eggs, and *very well* cooked grains should also pass with no trouble.

POISONINGS

Like a young child, a dog investigates everything with his mouth. And simply because he doesn't know that certain things aren't good for him, he'll try anything once. A child is more likely to swallow bleach, kerosene, or other caustic chemicals because of the human way of drinking: we first tilt our heads back and then pour the liquid into our mouths. This way, something can be on its way down the esophagus almost before we've had a chance to taste it. But with a dog, this isn't so likely to happen. He sniffs everything first and has to lap at liquids with his tongue. So unless they smell *and* taste good, he's not about to bother with them.

Unfortunately, one liquid that *does* taste good to a dog is automobile antifreeze—specifically, the ingredient ethylene glycol, which is sweet tasting and extremely poisonous. Symptoms of poisoning include drooling, vomiting, disorientation, and convulsions. Offer the dog wine or beer (alcohol is a specific antidote for ethylene glycol) and get him to the veterinarian's as fast as you can.

Rat poison works on rats—and your dog—by causing internal bleeding of the stomach and intestines. If you believe your pet has eaten rat poison, get him to the vet to have his stomach pumped, which is standard treatment for any poisoning or suspected poisoning. Some vets will advise you not to make the dog vomit, since the offending substance may be breathed in or may burn his throat on the way back up. But unless you can get to the vet's *fast,* we believe it's better to induce vomiting so that as little as possible of the poison gets into his system. Of course, if you know exactly what your dog has consumed, basic antidotes and treatments for human poisonings will work for him too. But if your pet comes home and starts acting strange, there's no way you can tell what he may have eaten. Two or three tablespoons of hydrogen peroxide or dry salt poured down your dog's throat will usually get him to throw up. And then, of course, an immediate visit to the vet is mandatory.

The possibility of poisoning is the best argument for teaching your dog never to rifle through garbage or to accept food without your approval. There are always slug baits, insect traps, and other lures set out for garden pests. A musician friend of ours took his two dachshunds to California with him. Accustomed to suburban New Jersey, the two dogs had a fine time roaming the hills of Topanga Canyon—until they came across a poisoned gopher carcass, left out by a local farmer trying to get rid of coyotes. Happily, their owner got them to a vet in time and had their stomachs pumped.

In addition, several hundred dogs are killed every year by *deliberate* poisoning, often in a neighborhood where some ill-trained dog or other has been barking, chasing cars, killing cats and pet rabbits, soiling lawns and sidewalks, and otherwise being obnoxious.

Dogs can get lead poisoning from chewing on old wooden furniture coated with lead-based paint. And another cause of canine poisoning is toxic houseplants. *Dieffenbachias,* philodendrons, and poinsettias can paralyze a dog's tongue and make it difficult for him to swallow. As a rule, it's safer not to grow such plants in any house with cats, dogs, or very young children.

SKIN PROBLEMS (DERMATITIS)

Your well-fed dog isn't likely to develop the sores associated with malnutrition unless he has some other problem in absorbing the required nutrients. (See Lick Granuloma—Hot Spots). Have your dog checked for worms, which are the usual culprits in a dog with nonitchy sores. Other possibilities include ringworm (which does not cause itching by itself) and cancer.

Some animals will display skin rashes as an allergic response, as Plum did when he ate the salami from the corner deli. To eliminate this possibility, cut out *all* extra tidbits and treats the animal is getting, from whatever source. Put him on a very high-quality, high-protein diet. (Eliminating or switching vegetables and grains may give you a clue, since once in a while a dog will develop allergies to one of these.)

Dry, scaly skin (seborrhea) often responds to extra polyunsaturated fats—up to 7 percent of the dog's total diet. Either have your veterinarian prescribe an appropriate supplement or add safflower or corn oil to your dog's regular food. Also make sure his diet contains plenty of the fat-soluble vitamins, especially vitamins E and F (linoleic acid). A vitamin and mineral supplement is important, too, to help plug any nutritional gap.

TRAVEL/MOTION SICKNESS

Travel sickness is one of the few instances where withholding food and water may be the only remedy. Ideally, a dog should be fed only *after* you've arrived wherever you're going. The presence of undigested food in his stomach is simply an invitation to motion sickness. For dogs who suffer chronically from nausea in the car, you might have your vet prescribe a sedative—but this is really a last resort, as it usually leaves the animal sleepy and disoriented.

You can accustom your pet to the car by taking him for short rides when he's a puppy. But air travel is another story. If the dog is going to be in a crate for a long flight in the cargo hold, you may want to provide him with some water to drink. At least one airline allows dogs to travel in the passenger compartment *if* they will fit into an eight-by-sixteen-by-twenty-one-inch traveling case, which effectively limits this privilege to Maltese spaniels, Chihuahuas, and other dogs standing less than eight inches at the shoulder. The animals must be back in their containers when food and beverages are served. (Remember, however, that a connecting flight you make may not extend the same privilege, and you may have to send your dog as cargo, after all.)

To get rid of extra energy and nervous tension, exercise your dog shortly before leaving for the airport. It's better to skip a meal entirely than risk stomach upset. Unless the weather is very warm, don't give a dog any water to drink within two hours of the flight, and *do* make sure he's walked one last time before leaving.

Few people realize that once an airliner is aloft, humidity of the pressurized air plummets dramatically. Therefore, your dog will definitely be thirsty when he disembarks. The low air pressure at high altitides can also hurt his ears and cause swelling of internal organs in some dogs—which is yet another argument for having their stomachs as empty as possible.

If you follow these troubleshooting guidelines, it's more than likely that your dog will live to a ripe and healthy old age. In a real sense, then, the best way to prepare for an animal's declining years is to keep him healthy *before them*. But when he grows older, diet and exercise can make even more of a difference in warding off (or at least forestalling) degenerative diseases.

12

Care and Feeding of the Aging Dog

 As a result of better medication and good nutrition, America's pet population now has a larger percentage of older dogs than ever before. And simply because veterinarians are seeing more aging dogs these days, they're becoming better equipped to care for particular geriatric problems.

By our definition, depending on the breed, a dog is "getting on" when he passes the age of about eight or nine years. This is the equivalent of the late forties or fifties in human terms. Folklore has it that one canine year is the equal of about six or seven human years. However, a recent study by the French Veterinary Academy determined that a one-year-old dog is physiologically as well developed as a fifteen-year-old human; but this equation changes as the dog grows older. (We have been saying this for years and first suggested it in *The Complete Book of Dog Training*.) You can figure on your dog being the equivalent of fifteen human years at one year, twenty-five years at two, and five years more for each subsequent year of life.

At first larger breeds mature more slowly than smaller dogs; but after the age of four or five, they start to age more quickly. Therefore, if your dog is one of the very large breeds, he's aging faster than an average-sized animal. In other words, if your Great Dane is eight years old, that's the equivalent of ten canine years for a smaller dog. So add 25 percent to a larger dog's age before calculating the human equivalent. Conversely, for very small dogs like Chihuahuas and dachshunds, you can subtract one canine year before consulting the human equivalent.

Your goal should be to keep your dog not just alive but *healthy* for as long as possible. And if you've been following the advice in this book, your task should be a lot easier. Certain diet changes can make an older dog a lot healthier and more comfortable, but the earlier you get him on a healthy diet, the longer he'll live, and the fewer problems he'll display along the way.

We don't have any magical eating plan that will spare your dog all the possible geriatric illnesses, but we do know that the regimen outlined in these pages is A1 as far as preventive medicine is concerned. All of our four dogs lived out their lives on this program, and all of them lived to ripe old ages: Plum to thirteen, Sleepy to fourteen and one-half and Inches to fifteen. (At age thirteen, Snap, our last Maltese, is helping us write this book.) Even in their later years, they were the best-behaved pets anyone could hope to enjoy, fitting perfectly into our lives and fulfilling all our expectations. We were able to take them with us everywhere—on a three-month camping trip, on plane flights, and down into the subways in carrying bags. There's no reason why every owner can't have dogs who are equally pleasurable and healthy.

AGING—A WORKABLE DEFINITION

Senility is the term most frequently used to refer to the mental and physical deterioration that occurs with old dogs. Aging is a progressive process in which there is a slow and sometimes steady wasting away of the animal's physical volume. The individual cells of the body become not only smaller, but fewer in number; in a very real sense, the animal is shrinking back toward the size he was when he was a young puppy. In general, most of the body processes slow down: cardiac efficiency may reduce by as much as 30 percent, kidney function by up to one-half of what it was. Metabolism usually limps along at four-fifths of its previous rate. Senile dementia, the mental side of senility, refers to the loss of intellectual faculties, including memory disorders, personality changes, deterioration in personal care, impaired reasoning, and disorientation. The problem with the word "senility" is that it is a catchall for all the mental and physical deterioration that occurs in old age. But you must check out each problem in your older dog; not every change is normal, and certain problems can be corrected with treatment. Especially now that so many advances in geriatric medicine have been made, you needn't allow your vet to be guilty of using senility as a general cover for all the ills of old age. Try to get to the root of the trouble and treat it.

THE GERIATRIC DIET

It's no wonder, then, that older animals of almost every species tend to be less active and more content to rest during a large part of the day. As a result, a dog's caloric requirements are lower. This means you should feed him fewer fats and carbohydrates than before. In fact, since fats are by nature less digestible than carbohydrates, it's best to cut them down to the bare minimum. Feed just enough to supply your aging dog with plenty of the unbankable fatty acids. (In short, switching entirely to poultry fat or vegetable oil is the way to go.) What carbohydrates you do give him can be cooked a bit longer now, to break down those starches completely.

At the same time, your dog needs plenty of micronutrients, especially the B vitamins, to help him metabolize those carbohydrates. Now is the time to stop overfeeding your dog and to adopt the "undernutrition" strategy, if you haven't been following advice and done so long before. Actually, your older dog doesn't need as many minerals as he did when he was a puppy—but since his ability to absorb them has diminished, its important to feed him at least as many as he was getting before.

Specifically, the aging dog needs plenty of vitamin A, the vitamin B complex (and perhaps B_{15}, which is reputed to combat degenerative disorders), and vitamin E and niacin for circulation. And since older dogs need to maintain strong bones, they need more calcium than when they were younger. It's important to give supplemental nutrients in balanced form, because deficiencies at this stage of life can result in premature senility. And, fortunately, proper nutrition can stave off problems of the liver, heart, and kidneys, which are all particularly vulnerable to age-related changes.

That 50 percent loss in kidney function means your older dog must go easy on protein. Because he isn't building up his tissues to any great extent, most of the proteins he does consume get metabolized for energy. But amino acids are broken down into nitrogen-rich urea, which the aging kidneys simply aren't able to eliminate as quickly or as easily as they could before. As a result, an old dog fed too much protein is likely to develop either an unhealthy level of urea in the blood or further impaired kidney function—or both.

On the other hand, scientists are discovering that protein deficiency in the older dog can manifest itself in tissue degeneration, anemia, weakness, accumulation of fluid in the tissues, and other problems. The answer, of course, is to feed your dog proteins with extremely high biological value that don't put stress on the kidneys by producing too much nitrogen which they would have to eliminate—gland meats, cooked eggs, chicken or turkey breast, and cottage cheese.

Appropriately low levels of protein, carbohydrates, and fats can be found in a number of special blends of dog food formulated especially for the geriatric dog. Be sure to check the labels very carefully, though; the contents of these blends vary widely from brand to brand. And lots more changes are likely. As more and more dogs reach their golden years, the dog food manufacturers are going to be presented with a widening market for specialized geriatric blends—and the competition can only increase. These blends already on the market, however, all presuppose that the dog who's eating them is basically healthy. If your dog has any problems (such as a heart or endocrine gland disorder), then your veterinarian should be able to prescribe a specific food that takes his liabilities into account.

One problem often noticed with older dogs is a general lack of appetite. It may be that the older dog's taste buds and olfactory nerves have become less effective, and the foods he used to enjoy now taste bland and less enticing. (If he's on a purposely bland therapeutic diet, of course, the problem is compounded.) You may want to use flavor supplements to keep your dog interested.

As one geriatric dog brochure puts it, "Frequency of feeding must be consistent; the same dietary patterns should be used each and every day." If a diet change can upset the system of a younger dog, it can wreak positive havoc on the older digestive tract. Because an aging dog's digestion slows, he may not be able to handle food "in one gulp" the way he used to; gastric juices, too, may have lower concentrations of enzymes and hydrochloric acid.

In fact, your older dog's eating habits may revert toward puppyhood. When our Inches reached the age of fourteen, he used to gobble down his meal and then throw it right back up. We cleaned it up, of course, but one day we were too slow and found him eagerly licking up what he'd regurgitated. The poet Wordsworth refers to "a dog returning to his vomit," a behavior trait that's been observed for centuries, but mostly in the case of young puppies who, as we explained in Chapter 4, may not be able to digest solid food too easily. This started us thinking—perhaps Inches hadn't been sick after all. We watched closely next time he ate. Sure enough, every so often, he would throw up a bit of food and then wolf it down again, just as a cow does with its cud. Once we began mushing down his food and adding extra water, he stopped this behavior completely. But when your older dog nears the age of ten or twelve, it may be necessary to go back to the morning-and-evening feeding schedule you'd use for a puppy, in order to compensate for his reduced digestive powers.

TOOTH LOSS AND ITS CONSEQUENCES

Although you can't tell how old a dog is by looking in his mouth, his teeth do wear down as he grows older. By the time he's eight or nine, he'll have lost the sharp points on his canine teeth and premolars; tartar will have stained some, or all, of the teeth a rusty color (the back molars in particular will be yellowish); and the gums will have receded somewhat, making the teeth (despite their wear) appear longer—hence comes the old expression, "long in the tooth."

If you've been following our advice and have been cleaning your dog's teeth by the procedures outlined in Chapter 11, they should stay in good condition. With age, however, tooth decay and gum disease are more prevalent. If tartar and plaque build up below the gum line, they can become a spawning ground for bacteria. The results are bad breath, the likelihood of infection and abscess, coupled with possible blood poisoning, causing kidney and heart problems. Some veterinarians recommend that dogs have their teeth cleaned professionally—a procedure that most veterinarians say has to be done under a general anesthesia. This is something we don't usually recommend.

Ask your veterinarian if he will administer a local anesthetic as some vets do. This method is easier to use if a dog is well-behaved, so if you have been cleaning his teeth regularly as we recommend, you will have gotten him used to having his teeth handled. He will therefore be a better candidate for local anesthesia.

If your dog's teeth are really rotten and perhaps need pulling, a general anesthetic may be the only solution. But before going this route, be sure your pet is in excellent health. A dog with a bad heart or a really old dog could be damaged or succumb. If your dog fits this category, just clean his teeth with a toothbrush daily as recommended and try scraping the tartar off with a tool such as a *very* dull butter knife. A tiny drop of clove oil put on the gum can calm an aching tooth, as can a buffered aspirin of the appropriate dosage, as will be discussed later in this chapter.

If a dog develops cavities or abscesses, usual practice is not to try to fill the affected teeth but just to pull them. Therefore, it's not at all unusual for an aging dog to have lost more or even all of his teeth either spontaneously or by extraction—as our Maltese Sleepy did in his old age. Even so, this doesn't necessarily mean you need to feed the dog nothing but liquids. If you use dry food, just soak it a little longer with extra added water and mash it up to make it softer. Or, keep him on the same canned dog food he's used to and mix a little water with it. If you mash up the food and add a little extra water, even a toothless dog can handle it quite well with his tongue and gums.

In fact, your entire house may be better off if you break up the older dog's food as much as you can.

When Snap was getting on and some of her teeth were missing, she decided the couch in our living room made a wonderfully comfortable dining table. She would tote chunks of food from her bowl to the pillows, where she could gum them slowly at her leisure. Even though we kept a close watch on her at feeding time, we began to realize we were losing the battle.

One afternoon, after picking crumbs of food off the suede for the umpteenth time, we got angry. When the next time came to feed Snap, we crushed her food into a thin layer at the bottom of her bowl and dumped in extra water so that it was the consistency of porridge. "There," Paul snorted, "if you can carry *this*, you can have the couch all to yourself!"

Since there was virtually nothing for her to pick up, Snap was forced to eat all of her dinner directly out of the dish. That, of course, was the answer that should have occurred to us long before. As a bonus, mashing dog food into pieces too small to carry also makes the meal far easier for an older dog to digest.

AGE ALERT

When your dog gets older, the hair around his muzzle will become gray—unless your dog is white or gray to begin with—and his eyes may take on a bluish or milky cast as the result of cataracts. He's now reached a stage when regular physical examinations including blood and urine tests can make a real difference. Any older dog should see a veterinarian twice a year at the very least; and if he's had any special health problems, a checkup every three or four months is preferable. Because your vet doesn't see your dog every day, he can quickly recognize small signs that you may have over-looked because they appeared so gradually.

That's why we advise all our clients to be especially observant around their pets—particularly as the dogs grow older. After many years of being with your dog, you'll have gotten to know his habits, both good and bad. At times, you'll be able to tell instinctively when something's wrong. If you do see suspicious behavior, check with your vet promptly. Ther are very few "owner hypochondriacs"; the problem is usually the reverse: simply because you have lived with your dog for so long, it's too easy to take him for granted. Any-one who's shepherded a dog through old age knows how guilt provoking and emotionally draining it can be when a veterinarian diagnoses some disorder whose symptoms were there all the time, if the owners had only noticed. It helps, then, to pay attention to your older dog, *expecting* to find certain changes. Groom him frequently, making sure you inspect beneath his hair for swellings, growths, and possible tumors.

Some older dogs can become deaf without your noticing it. At first, the dog may simply seem inatten-tive or disobedient; later, a few tests, such as speaking the dog's name in a low voice, will demonstrate that the dog simply can't hear you. Surgery to counteract failing hearing in an older dog is usually unnecessary, and always expensive. Loss of hearing as a dog ages is normal. Teaching your dog to respond to visual and hand signals at an early stage—or even before—is a far better solution. (See *The Complete Book of Dog Train-ing* and *Supertraining Your Dog.*)

An animal resembles its parents not only physically but also in the changes it goes through in life; if either of your dog's parents succumbed to a known ailment, that can suggest a similar vulnerability in your dog's genetic makeup. It always helps to ask a breeder about the parents' medical history—and if your dog has papers, the original breeder should still have this information.

Chronic cough may result from fluid in the lungs, this in turn, being a side effect of a weak heart and sluggish circulation. When Inches developed a heart condition, we first noticed something was wrong one day when he was sitting and gave a sudden jerk, as if startled or surprised. As it turned out, his heart had actually missed a beat. But with medication and proper diet, we were able to keep him alive and happy for another two years.

HEART AND KIDNEY PROBLEMS

Heart conditions, kidney disease, and hormonal disorders can be eased or arrested by proper drugs and diet; but all require special diets that your vet should prescribe. A dog with cardiac trouble needs a diet very low in sodium, which will probably be a boon for his kidneys as well. Sodium encourages a buildup of water in the body tissues, so cottage cheese, boiled, fresh fish, and poultry are better for the dog than meats that may contain a naturally high level of salt (kidneys, for instance). The heart trouble patient also needs more carbohydrates to make sure his heart muscle has plenty of energy.

An older dog's kidneys naturally weaken with age, and a smell of urine on the breath (other than in a nursing dog who's cleaning up after her puppies) is a sign of serious kidney disease. Basically, urea is not being filtered from the blood and is building to a point where it's being secreted through the salivary glands and mucus membranes. Kidney failure, unfortunately, is not reversible. That is, a kidney cannot be repaired or "improved" by medication; all you and the vet can hope to do is halt further deterioration. Being careful about the protein in your dog's diet is about all you can do.

Problems with the kidneys and heart have a direct effect on fluid levels elsewhere in the body. If the heart weakens, dissolved salts and blood plasma tend to accumulate in the tissues—a condition known as edema, or dropsy. Often such fluid buildup can occur in the lungs or abdomen and lead to pneumonia or other complications. In such a case, your veterinarian will probably prescribe diuretics, medicines that stimulate the kidneys to remove extra salts and fluid from the bloodstream. (This, of course, means that you'll have to give your pet oral medication; the method is detailed in Chapter 10). The best time to administer medicine is right before you feed your dog. That way, the stomach is geared up to receive the medicine, and if it's at all potent, the coming food will cushion its effects, avoid digestive upsets, and help metabolization.

But when it comes to diuretics, dogs manage to create one final dietary contradiction.

THE POTASSIUM PARADOX

Any medication may neutralize certain micronutrients. Dogs on medication in particular need vitamin supplements to replace whatever their dosages may have destroyed. Your vet should be able to warn you of any deficiencies that a given prescription can possibly cause. As just one example, diuretics will make the body lose potassium, among other minerals.

Potassium is a substance that plays a very important role in the working of muscles and the circulatory system. Unfortunately, your dog's kidneys treat it as just another salt, and excess urination can cause a potassium deficiency. According to a recent medical report, potassium deficiencies can in turn produce irreversible kidney damage and other impaired renal function. Regrettably, certain potassium supplements, which could seem to be the logical answer, can be dangerous. They are too concentrated for animal use and may cause irregular heart rhythms in dogs. (Of course, if a dog has weak kidneys, he must be given less than the recommended dosage anyway.) So with diuretics, it's safer to supplement a dog's diet with food that is rich in potassium—namely, blood meal, chicken, potatoes, and certain vegetables. (Vitamins and minerals may well also help prevent this buildup of toxic urea.)

If your older dog urinates or defecates indoors after years of obedient housetraining, this is not an automatic sign of senility—but it *does* need correction. The dog should be reprimanded, of course, but also the vet should check him to rule out kidney problems and any other medical alibis. As we said earlier, senility cannot explain away all old age problems. The onset of old-age diabetes can cause frequent urination, as can a hormone deficiency; and older female dogs occasionally dribble urine involuntarily, which is a treatable condition. A simple blood test and urinalysis will either pinpoint the problem or at least show what's *not* causing the urination. Also, an older dog, again like a puppy, may need to be walked more frequently, if only because the muscle tone of bowels and bladder aren't what they used to be.

TRAINING, EXERCISE, AND MOBILITY

Any dog is a creature of habit, but an older dog is even more so. Behavior patterns that have persisted for ten years and more are hard to alter, much less break. Thus, while your dog *can* learn new tricks, he's going to have trouble with lessons that contradict or modify what he already knows. For example, if your dog has been allowed on the furniture in the past, it'll be very difficult to keep him off the couch after he's twelve years old. If he was used to defecating in the back yard at six o'clock every evening, it may be hard to wean him to a different spot or a new time.

On the other hand, a brand-new trick (such as finding a treat or tidbit according to your hand signals) is a challenge that he can handle without too much confusion. But remember, an older dog lacks the sensory apparatus that makes the world seem strange and new when he's younger. Therefore, what would evoke curiosity in a young puppy may frighten and bewilder an older animal, if he notices at all. Not that he's seen it all before—he can't see it, period. After the age of thirteen or so, a dog will have definitely slowed down and may have trouble making new associations and remembering. A dog this age also needs a lot of attention. He will no longer have the energy to come bounding over for your approval, so it's only fair that you go to him. An older dog needs especially good pats and reassurance in the case of a move to a new house or some other drastic alteration of routine.

As the older dog's muscles diminish and his bones weaken, you should give him lighter, gentler exercise. Short, slow walks are more his style now. High jumps and long runs are fine for younger animals, but older dogs are prone to osteoarthritis, the same stiffening and calcification of the joints that afflicts aging humans. It's particularly important that the aging dog be slim and trim, since extra poundage can accelerate arthritic deterioration.

Dogs usually get arthritis in the hips more often than in the wrists or ankles. Thus, you won't see any knobbiness or malformation of the paw, as you would in the hands of a human artiritis victim. But you can observe the differences in behavior caused by pain: your older dog may be slow in getting up off the floor and will often be hesitant and tentative when it comes time to climb stairs. If the arthritis is indeed in the hips, the dog may appear duck-footed, holding his back legs tightly together, with his feet pointing out. And just as with humans, the arthritic pain is worse in damp weather. (In reality, humidity has nothing to do with it. Wet weather is more often associated with low air pressure, which in turn allows body tissues to swell, putting strain and pressure on inflamed joints. That's why arthritis sufferers often feel twinges before a rainstorm—because the barometer is already dropping, even though the weather is still dry.)

And just as with a human arthritis sufferer, you can give your dog aspirin—figure on one tablet per forty pounds of your dog's body weight. (A word of caution:

aspirin can cause an acid burn on your dog's esophagus if he doesn't swallow it properly. Try encasing it in cheese, peanut butter, or some other coating that will shield it at least until it reaches the stomach.)

In humans, aspirin has been shown to be effective in preventing heart attacks, so a regular daily dosage may actually do the older dog some good besides relieving arthritic pain. But because aspirin also has been associated with ulcers and internal bleeding, it's best to give the buffered kind, or, feed your dog a biscuit immediately afterwards to buffer the tablet and make sure it's on its way down. Lastly, remember that if your arthritic dog is getting less exercise, his nails may fail to wear down automatically and so may need clipping.

One of our clients was taking her Akita out through the lobby when the mailman greeted her and asked if the dog tended to walk close by the side of buildings: "I'd heard that Akitas will always walk right next to walls because they were originally bred to guard the Great Wall of China." This myth has no basis in fact. However, some dogs will "hug" a wall to obtain shade in very hot weather, as will aging dogs who no longer feel steady on their feet. Any animal who feels threatened will instinctively back itself up against a solid surface. Just as an aged human likes to have plenty of handholds, so does a solid surface on one side give an aging canine a sense of security.

Bibliography

American Kennel Club. *Obedience Regulations.* New York: American Kennel Club, Inc. (51 Madison Avenue, New York, N.Y. 10010), 1982.

Code of Federal Regulations 21–CFR (Sections 500 through 599, covering federal regulations for food and drugs for animals, and Section 501.101, covering regulations on pet food labeling). Washington, D.C.: U.S. Government Printing Office (Washington, D.C. 20402), 1983.

Faust, E. C. *Animal Agents and Vectors of Human Disease.* Philadelphia: Lea and Febiger, 1955.

The Gaines Corporation, Inc. *Basic Guide to Canine Nutrition.* White Plains, N.Y. Gaines Professional Services (250 North Street, White Plains, N.Y. 10625), 1977.

Kirk, Robert W., and Bisner, Stephen I. *Handbook of Veterinary Procedures and Emergency Treatment.* Philadelphia: W. B. Saunders Co., 1969.

Laurence Urdang Associates. *The Bantam Medical Dictionary.* New York: Bantam Books, Inc., 1981.

Loeb, Jo and Loeb, Paul. *The Complete Book of Dog Training.* New York: Pocket Books, Inc., 1977.

———. *Supertraining Your Dog.* Englewood Cliffs, N.J.: Prentice-Hall, Inc., 1980.

———. *You Can Train Your Cat.* New York: Simon & Schuster, 1977.

Bibliography

Mindell, Earl, and Mundis, Hester. *Earl Mindell's Vitamin Bible*. New York: Warner Books, Inc., 1979.

National Research Council, *Nutrient Requirements of Dogs*. Washington, D.C.: National Academy of Sciences, 1974.

Official Publication of the Association of American Feed Control Officials. Charleston, W.V.: Department of Agriculture (Room E-111, State Capitol Building, Charleston, W.V. 25305), 1983.

Index

A

Adams, Matthew, 4
Additives, 63, 68, 69, 202
  in dog biscuits, 78
Adolescent dogs, 77
Aerobics, 161
After-dinner walks, 164–
  65
Aging dogs, 21, 243–58
  being alert for prob-
    lems of, 251–53
  diet for, 110, 246–50
  flatulence in, 230
  heart and kidney prob-
    lems of, 253–54
  potassium for, 254–55
  training, exercise, and
    mobility of, 256–58
Aggressiveness, 142
  sugar and, 201–2
Akitas, 180
  exercise for, 163–64

Allergies, 230
  skin, 233, 240
American Kennel Club, 2
  Obedience Trials, 139,
    172
Amino acids, 41–42, 47
Anal scent glands, 133
  abcess of, 237
*Ancyclostoma duo-
  deneale,* 198
Anemia, 49
  from flea infestation,
    189
  from worms, 193, 196–
    97
Antibiotics, 210
  for bladder infections,
    122
  for salmonellosis, 137
  supplements and, 228–
    29
Antivitamins, 49–50, 158
Appetite loss, 221–22

How To Have a Happier & Healthier Pet

Paul Loeb and Josephine Banks, internationally acclaimed experts in animal behavior, have written classical guides to perfecting your pet's behavior and health.

Step-by-step, the authors explain practical and effective methods for:

Increasing your pet's obedience

Helping your dog become healthier and better behaved through diet and exercise

Teaching your pet good habits through love and understanding

Helping your pet accept strange places and new people.

☐ **THE COMPETE BOOK OF DOG TRAINING**
66657/$3.95

☐ **YOU CAN TRAIN YOUR CAT**
67182/$4.50

☐ **SUPERTRAINING YOUR DOG**
66666/$4.50

☐ **NUTRITION AND YOUR DOG**
67868/$4.50

POCKET
B O O K S

Simon & Schuster Mail Order Dept. ICS
200 Old Tappan Rd., Old Tappan, N.J. 07675

Please send me the books I have checked above. I am enclosing $_____ (please add 75¢ to cover postage and handling for each order. N.Y.S. and N.Y.C. residents please add appropriate sales tax). Send check or money order—no cash or C.O.D.'s please. Allow up to six weeks for delivery. For purchases over $10.00 you may use VISA: card number, expiration date and customer signature must be included.

Name_____

Address_____

City_____ State/Zip_____

VISA Card No._____ Exp. Date_____

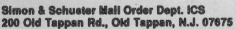

Signature_____215